# Little Girl Arise

## Tarkisha Wallace, LPC-S

Printed in the United States of America.

First Printing, 2018

ISBN 9-7817202688-7-1

Soar Publishing

1443 Delplaza Drive.

Baton Rouge, LA 70815

# Dedication

Little Girl Arise is dedicated to the person who completely changed my life on October 29, 2005, but departed soon after, leaving an impression that would last a lifetime. There is no greater way to celebrate your 13th birthday than dedicating this project to you. Jayden Charles Wallace, your mommy, misses you, loves you, and awaits the reunion we will one day have in heaven. Until then, continue cheering mommy on as I strive to fulfill the purpose for which God created me. As promised, I haven't and will never forget!

Happy 13th Birthday Jayden!

-Mommy

# Acknowledgements

Jeremiah 29:11 reads, "For I know the thoughts that I think toward you, says the Lord, thoughts of peace and not of evil, to give you a future and a hope."

To know that before I was created, before being born, having an identity, starting school, or securing a job, God had thoughts of purpose, success, and greatness concerning my life. Before I ever knew myself, He knew exactly who I was, and created a purpose specifically for me. It goes without saying, Your plans have proven to supersede my own in every way imaginable. I acknowledge, honor, and reverence You for who You are to me now, who You'll be to me in the future, and who You've been to me since the day I loss my son. God, You're all-knowing, You've done things very intentionally, and You've ensured that as long as I remain aligned with Your will, all things have and will continue to work together for my good (Romans 8:28). For every "no," every valley experience, and every time You didn't allow me to have my way, Thank You. For every gift and talent, every success, and every natural reward and recognition, Thank You. In return, I hope to make You smile.

Parenting me was not an easy job, but someone had to do it. William "Cookie" and Karen did an outstanding job with the resources and knowledge they had to raise my sisters and me to be the women we've grown to be. My parents made sure of a few things: we knew God, we knew discipline, we knew love, and we knew the value of education. Of course, I wasn't jumping for joy when it was time for consequences for my actions, but the value in those lessons have yielded great results as an adult. Mama and Daddy, if I could package all your wants and dreams into a box, and have it specially delivered to you, know that I would. I appreciate the morals and values you've both instilled in me, without those, I am positive I wouldn't have had the wherewithal to survive the storms I've weathered and maintained my sanity.

Thank you for the support you continuously show me. Thank you for being my defense and my protection. Losing Jayden was difficult for each of us. It impacted our lives drastically; however, you both put aside what you were experiencing to make sure I had what I needed to push through. I am tremendously grateful for the two of you, the God in you, the guidance you continue to provide, and the love you pour into your girls.

To my living grandparents. I am forever thankful for the way you made me feel when I was a child, which helped mold me into an adult. Though there's probably no truth to this, I tell everyone when growing up Kellie was daddy's favorite, Ebony was mama's favorite, and I was our grandparents' favorite. You each knew how to make me feel like a big girl then and even more so now. Papa Robert, you make it crystal clear how big I am in your eyes and how proud you are of me, thank you. Granny, you know just what to say to bring a smile and a laugh, "oh a man huh?" I know you'll get that. I love you both so much.

It doesn't get any better than the Wallace Girls'. To my sisters, there's so much I could say, but I must keep it brief. Y'all two are absolutely everything to me. I'm tremendously grateful that when God planned out our lives, He connected the three of us. The world must know, we're a package deal; if you want one, you get all three, and in my opinion, that's a deal worth having. I am honored to be your big sister, support, friend, soror, and everything else we've been and one day will be to one another. Ebony and Kellie, thank you for standing with me through every low and high moment, every success and failure, every joyous occasion and bad breakup, and every new venture; always supporting me along the way. Where I lack y'all pickup, and where y'all come up short, y'all know I'm here. Thanks for being the true definition of sisters; I'm almost positive they don't make them like us anymore.

To my favorite little people David, Kent, Payton, and Brook, never forget this, and don't let anyone tell you differently, I love each one of you the most! And I mean it, the most!! My world is full because of my little brother, nephew, and two nieces. The love, smiles, and excitement y'all genuinely display towards me helps ease a pain that you may not even know exists. This world is yours, and I'm here to make sure of it. Every opportunity, every dream, every win! I love y'all.

To my best friend, Tamika, thank you! You have been a source of support since Spring 2004. Two different women from completely different worlds, came together like we grew up in the same home; we've been Mek and Kisha ever since. We've watched each other cry our eyes out, suffer and struggle, accept less than what we were worth or deserved, recover from it all, accomplish very high goals, and grow to be women who are well aware of our purpose and determined to fulfill it. Since November 2, 2005, one thing you've consistently done was remind me of my strength. You'd frequently say, "Kish, you're the strongest person I know, you're going to make it through this." No matter what trial I was facing, you reminded me of what I survived and reassured me that I'd make it through that too. I can't thank you enough for exceeding what a standard friendship looks like to help nurture and grow the bond we share. You know me and love me, in spite of my flaws! You've never judged me and always support me; I am beyond blessed to call you friend, best friend that is!

To every person that lived those five long days (October 29 – November 2, 2005) with me and have walked with me through the hurt and thereafter. If I've never said it before, thank you!

To three amazing Arisen Little Girls, Hope Coleman, Crystal Ezeff, and Erin Meyers, thank you! Because of each of you, many little girls will begin to arise.

To my Ghostwriter and National Best-Selling Author, Lorna A. Lewis, thank you! Little Girl Arise was an idea sitting in my email and notes on my phone until you posted a status on social media. Thank you for being obedient and dedicated to your calling. Within the past few months, you've pushed me, prayed for me, encouraged me, and didn't allow me to quit. When you noticed it was difficult, you checked in, when you saw I was moving slow, you checked in; you fulfilled the role you promised to play, and for that I'm grateful. You weren't the Ghostwriter I joked about, but you were the Ghostwriter intended for me. Your question, "Do you know my line name is Ghostwriter?" was all the confirmation I needed. Writing and coaching are not only your talent but clearly they're your gift. I'm excited to see what the rest of the world gains from Changing Lives the Write Way.

To my family and friends, my Strong Friends, my goddaughters, Delta Sigma Theta Sorority, Inc. (my line sisters, neos, and sorors), my church family, and my colleagues, clients, mentors, and mentees. To every person that believes in me and the gift God placed on the inside of me. To every person praying for and covering me... thank you! Know this, I see and feel every bit of love, support, and encouragement, and it's greatly appreciated. I love each of you.

-Tarkisha

# Foreword

WOW! Life is full of surprises, and this is definitely a welcomed one. My prayers for Tarkisha have been answered far above anything I could've thought or imagined. God is so good!

Watching her life unfold before me is one of the greatest blessings I've received from the Lord. I remember her taking her first steps. She was so excited and full of laughter. I watched her fall and get back up time after time erupting with laughter each round. Without ever being told to get up and try again, she repeatedly got up and walked. Little did I know that was the beginning of my little girl's arising.

Seeing her develop and blossom into the woman she has become is a complete blessing. Her father and I both are very grateful to God for allowing us the task of parenting our first of three daughters. Though there were many challenges, the blessings and joy exceed them all. Her role as the oldest child and big sister to her siblings was always loving and supportive. She possessed characteristics of good morals and talent and set high standards for her sisters to follow.

The leadership qualities she has demonstrated throughout her youth, catapulted her into a career of directing a team of professionals, opening her own counseling and consulting business, and now the author of this wonderful book entitled *Little Girl Arise*.

Bishop T.D. Jakes said it this way, *"Some little girl needs to know your recipe for survival. Somewhere in the world there is a little girl dying because she does not know that it is possible to survive what you have already endured."*

In 2005, I witnessed Tarkisha go through a very traumatic experience. As her mother, I felt so helpless because I couldn't take away the pain she was experiencing. The family rallied together in a time of fasting and prayer, seeking God for strength for Tarkisha, and a miracle for her son, Jayden. Prayer is something the Wallace family was very acquainted with. God's answer to our prayers was to bring Jayden back to Heaven, and although it was not the answer that we wanted, He sustained Tarkisha through one of what I believe was the darkest seasons of her life. Out of that traumatic experience *Little Girl Arise* was birthed.

*Little Girl Arise* is a testimony and a tool to help *little girls* all over the world arise from their places of pain and move into their purpose and the destiny that God has designed for them. Revelation 12:11 says, *"They overcame him by the blood of the Lamb and by the word of their testimony."* My prayer is that every *little girl* who reads this book will overcome every painful experience of the past and *arise* as the virtuous woman God created them to be.

Karen
A Mother Who Prays!

Mark 5:41 - "Then He took the child by the hand, and said to her, 'Talitha, cumi,' which is translated, 'Little Girl, I say to you, arise.'"

# Little Girl Arise

## Introduction

I'm writing this to share a *real-life* journey of pain that led me to my purpose. After many life experiences, now, while in the midst of a situation that at times feels unbearable, I say to God, *"as long as this pain comes wrapped in purpose I'll endure."* I'm writing this because after my first *dying* experience, I faced many more. None nearly as painful as the one I'd previously experienced, but still piercing. My purpose is to encourage, inspire, motivate, and cover each *Little Girl* as she prepares to *arise*.

And for those who are not ready, I'm writing this to wait with you, support you, be a listening ear for you; a model for you, and to cover you because *arising* after such fatal events takes courage. It takes strength. It takes love and support. And sometimes it takes knowing that someone else just like, or similar to you, is living again too. Knowing that another woman conquered what once tried to conquer you may help you realize that you are more than a conqueror.

There's nothing that makes me more special than anyone else. Nothing that would cause God to single me out. He wants to extend the same grace and mercy to you. He wants to use your life to help *Little Girls* connected to you encounter their *arising* moment as well.

Along with this book is a workbook component. As you read, there will be times you're asked to take a moment and reflect. There will be times you'll be asked to engage in an activity associated with the chapter you're reading. Taking advantage of each of these opportunities is of great importance to your *arising*.

As a believer and a counselor, I know that as God reveals things to us, we have to put them into practice; we have to strategize, plan, prepare, and most importantly, pray. He has led me to use this as a tool to help us in each area. I pray that this book blesses you the way it blessed me. I pray that it honors God, and helps you understand that His intentions for you are far greater than you can imagine. I pray that you'll use this book as a tool to help you move towards your purpose. I hope that the *little girl* inside of you gets the nudge and *arises.* Before we begin, allow me to cover our journey together in prayer.

Father God,

As I, once a *little girl* myself, embark upon this journey to share with Your daughters, I ask that You prepare their minds and open their hearts to receive the amazing things You have in store for them. Take me out of the equation and have them only see and focus on You.

I ask now, that You will do a work in the lives of Your daughters--Your *little girls* as they read the words that You've spoken through me. I ask that You'll move abundantly in them in a way that they may have felt would never happen for them. Spark change in them that they've resisted. Reignite fire in them that's dimmed down to less than a flicker. Restore faith, hope, courage, and love. I pray that as the words come off the pages, restoration begins for each of them. Most of all I pray that forgiveness happens, so they're made whole, and healing may begin.

I thank You that we're challenged to be bigger, better, and stronger. I thank You that we're motivated to change our ways and commit to Yours. I pray that we not only go along with Your plan for our lives, but that we align and stand in total agreement with it. I thank You that we gain revelation, and acknowledge, accept, and begin to live out our purpose in You. But Father, we need You to do it! We need You to create it. We need You to remain with us through it.

I ask that You use my journey for the intent You had when You created me. I pray that the women who are suffering, the generation that's dying, and everyone in the world who's lost their faith, will look at my life and be reminded of a God, that loves us and has great things for us. I pray You'll use all that I've experienced, all that hurt me, and all that I thought was meant to destroy me, to get me to the exact place that You desire for me. I pray You'll thrust me into Your purpose for my life.

Thank You Lord for choosing Your stubborn daughter, Your, sometimes, disobedient daughter, Your hurting daughter.

You knew who I was, and You've helped me to acknowledge who I am as well. Do the same for *little girls* everywhere. I love You

# Little Girl Arise

for all that You will do for each *little girl* that reads this book. Father, I pray that we clearly hear Your voice speaking, *"Little Girl, I say to you, arise."*

In Jesus Name. Amen

# *Chapter 1:*

# *Pain*

How did this happen? How did a normal day end with me confined to a hospital bed in Labor and Delivery two months before my actual due date? For several days my sorors, frat brothers, and friends checked on me. I knew my family would've been there if they could, but they were all in Baton Rouge, and I was here in Natchitoches, Louisiana, without the people I needed the most. I slept in that cold room alone each night trying to figure out what was going on in my body. A hospital stay isn't something a person wants to do alone, especially with the battle I was now fighting.

Perhaps it'll help to tell you how this part of my story began. It was March 2005, three months shy of graduating with my bachelor's degree, I had a lot going on during that time. Preparing for graduation, hanging out with my sorors and friends, and of course my *love* life. Even though every minute of my life was filled with something, it wasn't enough to keep me from noticing how my body was unexpectedly changing.

I'm sure you're thinking this is the part where I went to the doctor to find out what was going on, right? Wrong. I was in my 20's, living what one might say was my best life, and I couldn't allow a minor body change to slow me down. I had *important* things to do, which is why my sorors and I were in Ruston for the weekend. There were Greek festivities, and I was determined not to miss out on anything. The only problem was, I couldn't enjoy myself the way I desired, because I felt weird. That's the only way I can describe it.

I tried as best as I could to ignore it, but eventually I couldn't hide it any longer. I had to say something. I mentioned it to a few of my friends, and they gave me "the look." You know, the exaggerated *giiiiiiirrrrrrlllllllll* look? That's the look they gave me, and I knew what they were insinuating, but they were wrong, which is why I brushed them off and finished my weekend. As soon as I returned home however, the welcomed distraction from the weekend was over, and the thought I dreaded most flooded my mind, *this may really be happening.*

The next day, I couldn't take it anymore. I knew what I needed to do and putting it off was no longer an option. I drove to Wal-Mart and felt as if I was about to do something very wrong; shame set in, but at this point, I had no choice. I discreetly purchased a pregnancy test and prayed all the way home. It was a must that the results returned negative. You'd have to know my mom to understand how extremely difficult it'd be for me to tell her that I was pregnant. Yes, I was *grown*, but I was still her child and being grown, pregnant, and unmarried went against everything she taught me. On top of that, years ago I made a purity vow to God, and as you've probably already guessed, I broke it, and now everyone else would know too. All of that went through my mind as I hurried inside my apartment holding the box that was about to determine my future. I gathered myself, took a deep breath, whispered another quick prayer, and then followed the instructions on the box.

*"Time has stopped,"* I thought, as I waited for the results. Surely, it shouldn't have taken this long, but the longer I waited, the more anxious I became. *"Would this thing come on? Hurry up and show me."* More time passed and still nothing. No negative. No positive. No nothing. Could this be a sign from God? Was this His way of telling me I'm not pregnant and I should ignore what I'm feeling and go on with my life?

*"Girl, you better get another test and do it again. You need to be sure, not just guessing."* Tamika, my best friend, obviously wasn't feeling the same sign from God as I'd felt hours ago. I wanted to protest, but I knew she was right, so there I was driving back to Wal-Mart, doing my walk of shame down the aisle with the pregnancy tests. I grabbed two tests and hurried to check out. Once again, I found myself sitting in the bathroom with my fate sitting on the counter. I entered the bathroom as a young lady, only responsible for myself and my well-being, but I walked out as a soon-to-be mom, now responsible for myself and the new life that was growing inside of me.

I was in complete disbelief. Twenty-one years old, three months shy of a bachelor's degree, with a boyfriend, now the father of my unborn child, who possessed all the qualities my mother disapproved of for her daughter. Guess none of that mattered since I wasn't even speaking to him. He wasn't there, and I had no plans to tell him. I was prepared to do this on my own.

I took the next few days to process everything that was going on, at least that's the excuse I told myself as to why I hadn't shared the news with my mom yet. But alas, there was no need stalling any longer. I needed to tell her and get it over with, and that's what I did. I would say that the conversation went horrible, but that would be putting it mildly; it went much worse than that... *MUCH WORSE*. She didn't say, *"Okay Kisha; it's going to be alright."* Nope. Not my mom. She doesn't believe in sugarcoating anything, even if it'll make you feel better. My mom is a tough love kind of person, and I don't think anyone experienced her tough love more than me.

I didn't get it at the time, but as I grew older, and a tad bit wiser, I understood why my mom treated me the way she did. Being my mom, she knew something I didn't know. She knew God placed something special on the inside of me and she was carrying out her responsibility as my mother to protect that gift. I also didn't understand the unimaginable pain that would greet me ahead and how that pain would be used to expose my gift to the world.

# Little Girl Arise

## Chapter 2:

### Painful Memories

I'd finally come to grips with my new normal, and then September came. I was eight months pregnant, thirty-two weeks to be exact, and I began to experience pain like nothing I'd felt before. *Dang, if these are Braxton Hicks contractions, I don't want the real deal,* I remember thinking. Have you ever been warned to be careful of the words you speak? Take heed to that warning.

Despite my pain, I went to work anyway. Everything I felt on the inside must've shown on my face because as soon as I walked in the door, my coworkers immediately turned me around and led me right back out. They suggested that I see my doctor immediately; I listened. I expected him to monitor me for a while then send me on my way. He did just that, except sending me on my way meant sending me straight to the hospital to be admitted. I was having real contractions, not Braxton hicks.

Preterm labor was not on my agenda that day, but that's what landed me in the hospital for five days. Thankfully my prayers worked, and the contractions stopped. My baby was fine, I was fine, and my mom, dad, and sisters were there to take me home. Leaving Natchitoches and all my friends wasn't the plan, but since my doctor diagnosed me as a high-risk pregnancy he ordered strict bed rest for the remainder of my pregnancy; my family felt moving back to Baton Rouge was best. I intended to stay until I delivered my family's first baby boy, and then we'd move back to Natchitoches. Well, you know what they say about the best-laid plans. My stay in Baton Rouge lasted longer than I expected, and the time leading up to my delivery (what should've been the happiest time of my life), ended up becoming my worst nightmare.

My friends in Natchitoches had planned my baby shower, and they insisted I come back. I would say it was peer pressure that made me go against my doctor's orders and my mother's advisement and go back to Natchitoches, but I'd be lying. As badly as they wanted me to come, I wanted to go.

"This isn't a good idea. You need to stay home and rest," my mom protested.

Maybe she was right, besides I was in physical therapy for my back and I could barely sit for thirty minutes without pain. Would I be able to make this trip? Of course, I can. Why'd I think I could do it? Because I now was twenty-two-years-old, and despite all the warnings from my mom, I had it all figured out. I believe that's called being hard headed!

I gave my friends the green light to come and get me. I stayed for two nights, enjoyed my shower, and was set to return home on Friday. The plan was for my boyfriend to drive me back. Yes, the inconsistent, rarely follow-through on anything boyfriend. Yes, the boyfriend that had proven time and time again that he wasn't dependable. That's the boyfriend I thought would drive me home. He never showed up. Big surprise!

Let me say this, it's not my intention to lead anyone to think my boyfriend was such a horrible, god-awful person. That would then pose the question, *well why was she with him anyway?* I knew without a doubt that my child's father loved me; that was never a question. He loved me and took fairly good care of me, financially. I rarely had a want that went unmet, and always felt protected and safe. Unfortunately, he proved time and time again that it was too hard for him to physically be there to take care of his pregnant girlfriend and *work* at the same time. He was a professional pharmacist, just not the legal kind. I don't know why, but I liked *bad boys*. Let me pause to thank God for deliverance.

Now back to that that night in Natchitoches, with him not showing up, I decided to wait and leave very early the next morning. This way I could take my time and stop every thirty minutes or so to give my back a rest. Did I mention that I wasn't supposed to be driving at all? I had no choice. I put myself in that situation, so I had to deal with the consequences. This trip wasn't ending on a good note, and little did I know, it was about to get so much worse.

Later that evening, I went to the bathroom at my best friend's apartment. Something wasn't right. Panicking, I contacted my doctor's after-hours nurse in Baton Rouge. She reassured me all was well, but it didn't feel like all was well to me. I called my cousin, who at the time was an LPN studying to be a RN. She advised me to get assessed, and that needed to happen that night in Baton Rouge, not Natchitoches.

I arrived in Baton Rouge early the next morning. I stopped at my mom's house to get my medical records. As we were leaving, my cousin stopped and looked back at my mom who was still standing in the same place I found her.

"Come on KayKay." My cousin motioned for my mom to follow us.

My mom looked at her and sternly responded, "I'm not going to the hospital. Nothing's wrong. Kisha will be okay. She needs to learn to listen. She doesn't know everything. I told her not to go. Y'all can take her, but I'm not going."

About ninety-nine percent of the time, when my mother says something she means it, and this time was no different. There was no time to try and change her mind--not that we could anyway; I just needed to get to the hospital.

We arrived for my check-up, which unexpectedly resulted in admission. I was checked in and placed on a monitor. My cousin and I got as comfortable as we could get in a hospital room with monitors beeping all around us and the inside temperature set on winter. My body was tired, and I'd finally closed my eyes, but that was short lived. Thirty minutes later, the nurse walked in and stood next to my bed.

"Alright, we're about to have a baby," she announced.

I looked around to see who she was talking to. Clearly, she was in the wrong room. Guess she was just as tired as I was.

I laughed at her mistake. "I'm not due until next month, they're just monitoring me," I explained. I waited for her to apologize for the mix-up and leave to find her real patient, but she didn't move nor, did she apologize. Instead, she corrected me.

"I know, but we're going to go ahead and take him. There's nothing to worry about. It's just that you've been on the monitor for about thirty minutes, and he hasn't moved. We think he may be in a sleep cycle, but Dr. Harris wants to take him just to be sure. It'll be fine."

To this day, I can clearly hear her words as if she'd just spoken them. It was the morning of October 29, 2005. I looked over at my cousin, who was just as shocked by the announcement as I was, and gave one simple, yet very important request. "Call my mom."

Things move quickly in labor and delivery. I was prepped for surgery and on the table awaiting my doctor who would be the first to introduce me to my *Little Man*. And guess who was there, bedside, by the time my doctor arrived. My mom! Normally, a drive from my mom's house to the hospital would take at least twenty minutes, maybe a little more if I take in consideration the red lights, but she made it in half the time. Years later she told me she must've made it there on wings. My mom may be tough, but when her children are in trouble, she's coming, and nothing will hinder her.

The surgery ended almost as quickly as it started. I heard the *awws* and *ooohhhs* around the room, but what I didn't hear was a cry. Every baby cry after delivery, so I waited and waited; I wanted to hear that cry. Maybe in the days to come less crying would be appreciated, but at that moment, to solidify his arrival, I wanted to hear, for the very first time, the sound of the one I carried.

My doctor looked at me. "Everything's fine. He had a bowel movement right before delivery, so I'm not letting him cry. I want to get him cleaned up, so he doesn't inhale it then we'll let him cry."

There are times when minutes feel more like hours, and this was one of those times. While still waiting, I left labor and delivery and was placed in the recovery room, still not hearing anything, barely seeing him, and not even getting the chance to hold him. I was so medicated but medicated or not I knew how this was supposed to go. I saw enough television shows to know how this worked. I was supposed to hear him cry, then they were to lay him on my chest. None of that happened. TV lied. In my experience, that's not how it happened at all.

Finally waking up from the sleep of all the medicine, I was greeted with a room full of people. Some I expected to see. Some I didn't even know, like the surgeon and a specialist who came to provide me with the status of my newborn little boy. The only thing was, I wasn't looking for a status, I was looking for Jayden; you know the baby they took out of me a little while ago. The baby I carried from February to October. The little boy that caused all those back problems and weight gain. I was looking for him. Not a specialist, not a surgeon, not anyone but him.

The doctors shared a lot of information, and I didn't understand most of it because my mind was in such a fog. Too much was happening at once. I tried to stay focused, and I'm sure I missed a lot, but two words I didn't miss were *life support*.

"Do you want to keep him on life support or let him expire?" The question repeatedly replayed in my head. It took me a minute to comprehend what they were asking me.

I finally found the strength to open my mouth and make my request known. *Today I'm saying request, but it was a demand.* "Put him on life support. I believe in God, I trust God will heal my baby, and he will live." I stated that with more assurance than I've ever been of anything in my life. Even though the doctors believed there was no chance of Jayden pulling through, and thought it was best for me to let him go, I couldn't. My faith told me to hold on a little longer.

None of this made sense. How did we get here? What went wrong? Just three days prior, at my doctor's visit, everything was great; this had to be a mistake. Maybe they switched him and gave me the wrong baby. That's possible. It's happened before. Unfortunately, they didn't have the wrong baby. He wasn't switched. It was my baby, Jayden Charles Wallace, who was born Saturday, October 29, 2005, at five o'clock in the morning, weighing six pounds, nineteen inches long, beautiful as can be. My baby who'd just made his entrance, was threatening to make his departure.

*Oh, no! Devil you will not have my son.* I was raised knowing the Word, so I went to it. I cried out to God; I begged God. I cried to my parents, my sisters, my friends, everyone except the person who should've been going through this with me,

Jayden's father. I cried to anyone who would listen. I knew what to do, but it wasn't working; not fast enough anyway. *Lord, they want to take the baby You gave me off the machine. You must step in. You must change this situation. What's going on? This isn't how this is supposed to go. You wouldn't give me a baby only to take him back the same day. God, please show up now for my little man.*

I asked for prayers, said prayers, played worship music, visited him in the NICU at Woman's Hospital, prayed over him, sang to him, but nothing worked. A baby who had a very strong, normal heartbeat just days before delivery. It didn't make sense, *Umm, where are you in this God? Why would you bless me with this baby, allow me to carry him full term, and give birth to him and then take him away from me? From my family? What's Your point? Help me to understand.*

I decided I needed to reframe my thinking. *God is going to use this for something. He needs seven days, and Jayden will be fine, just seven days.* I tried to explain that to the specialist who visited with me on November 2nd, four days later.

"The test I ran determined that he won't recover. I'm 100% sure of that," she stated.

I watched as she spoke, but her words meant nothing. God would have the final say.

"If by any chance he does pull through, he'll be a vegetable his entire life," she continued.

I knew she meant well, but she didn't know what I knew. I was his mother, and it was my job to protect my son.

"Leave him on, God needs two more days that's all."

Her sympathetic look aggravated me. "Baby God doesn't need a ventilator," she softly responded.

*Don't tell me what God needs. Don't take him off.* At this point, I was angry and furious. She didn't get it, and nothing I said mattered, so I said nothing more.

Later that day I had a room full of visitors. My doctor felt it was a strong possibility my son wouldn't make it through the day. She thought it would be better if I was discharged and home with my family. I may have been going home, but I planned to return every day to visit my baby, because he was *not* going to die. God just needed more time.

While having a silent visit with my guests, my mom called. After hearing I'd be discharged, she went home to get my room ready for me. We talked for a moment, and then the question came. The one I didn't want to entertain.

"Kisha, have you thought about it yet, have you made a decision?" My mom asked.

"No." I firmly responded

*"Is Pastor still there?"* She asked.

"Yes," I replied. I knew where this was going, and I didn't like it.

"Ask everyone to leave and talk to Pastor," my mother said. I was quiet, and then with the words I dreaded hearing, she continued, "You have a beautiful baby. Send Jayden back to God the way God sent him to you. It's time."

I heard everything my mother said, but like many times before, I didn't agree with her. Nevertheless, as she advised, I poured out my heart to Pastor explaining that I just couldn't let my son go; I couldn't let him die. I didn't want him to die, and I surely didn't want to be the person to make the most difficult decision any parent could be asked to make. I expressed to him the same thing I'd already told everyone else, God needed more time. I couldn't rush Him with something as fragile and important as the life of my five-day-old baby boy. It's amazing how I was willing to wait on God then but want to rush Him with everything else now.

Pastor allowed me to have my say before he finally spoke. "When you release Jayden back to God you'll have your own personal cheerleader in heaven. You'll have someone pulling for you, saying, *'mommy, you can do it,'* But you have to release him first."

Those words touched me, they still do, but even that wasn't enough.

*Why can't Jayden stay here and cheer?* I wanted to ask but didn't. I figured he'd be more helpful cheering me on here than from heaven, but I was done. I didn't have any more fight in me. It was painfully clear that everyone else saw and knew something I didn't see. Couldn't see. Or just refused to accept until now.

Later that day, I went to the Neonatal Intensive Care Unit and held my baby for the first time. That afternoon I sat with Jayden for hours. Nine months of carrying him, five days of watching him, and I was finally able to hold him. I held him feeling an overwhelming sense of peace, a lot of hurt and resentment, but still, there was peace.

Confusion, but peace. Anger, but peace. Disappointment, but peace. Disadvantaged, but peace. Guilt, but peace. *God's peace.*

It was truly a peace that surpassed all understanding (Philippians 4:7). I felt this peace before, about two or three days earlier, but I misunderstood it. I thought that peaceful feeling meant Jayden would recover. Now I understand that God gave me that peace as a reminder that in the midst of pain, disappointment, anger, confusion, and even *death*, He's still there. He was with me. And during your pain-provoking and dying situation, He's with you.

I prepared to leave the NIC Unit and told the nurse the hardest thing I ever had to say. "You can remove him from the machine. If he dies okay, but maybe he'll live." Even though I consented, I still had hope that God would work a miracle and my baby would live.

A couple hours later the nurse called to inform me that my son, my precious little boy, my little man, had passed away.

"It took him a while to pass because he had a very strong heartbeat, but he went peacefully." Every word she spoke chipped away at my heart and in that moment, I'd gone from a hopeful mom to a grieving mom. All of it made no sense to me; a beautiful, normal, healthy-to-the-eye baby died. How could this be? As bad as it may sound, I felt like I'd wasted nine months being pregnant only to leave the hospital and go home empty-handed. I was done, done, done. November 2, 2005, my little man, my baby boy, Jayden (whose name means *God Has Heard*) Charles Wallace, died, and so did I; only, I was left here to suffer in the pain of his actual death and my own emotional, mental, and spiritual *death*.

# Little Girl Arise

## Chapter 3:

### Working Through the Pain

I wish I could tell you about the major events that occurred in my life after my son died. I'm sure there were many, but I wouldn't know because for years after his death, my life was a blur; the only thing I remember well was the pain. That excruciating pain, the kind that no matter what I did, nothing helped. It had become a familiar feeling. Hurting quickly became *normal* for me. I was angry, bitter, and depressed. I wanted my precious little boy back, and since that wasn't happening, I wanted answers…I *needed* answers. God had to tell me something to make me understand.

Actually, there are some major events I remember quite well. The birth of my nieces and nephew. I watched each of them enter the world. Each time felt just as miraculous as the first. I celebrated with my sisters, but as you can imagine, their happy beginning was a painful reminder of my tragic ending. I stood strong for my sisters in labor and delivery. Even in recovery, I was there for whatever they needed. I always wanted to be an aunt so of course I was excited about each birth, but unfortunately, that excitement wouldn't follow me, because once I'd leave the hospital, I'd go home and cry.

My middle sister, Ebony, texted me that evening after giving birth to her first child. She thanked me and acknowledged how strong I was in the delivery room. She knew it wasn't easy for me, but we're sisters, if she needs me, I'm there. I called my mom to share a very open and honest moment with her. I simply said, "Ma, I'm not jealous. It just hurts. I don't understand why God did this to me. I don't understand why he took my son." Sometimes I still don't know, and there are times like now, I remember and can physically feel the pain I felt all those years ago. Pain that would follow me until I birthed Jayden again, I know that makes no sense, but keep reading, and you'll understand the second birth. The one that allowed me to birth him to finally release him.

I've endured things I never imagined. Hurt, disappointment, rejection. I used to find myself asking, "God, haven't I suffered enough?" Then one day a guy I was dating unapologetically helped open my eyes to the role I'd been playing in my suffering. He informed me how offensive and impolite I came off to others, especially to him. He brought to my attention that at times others didn't want to be around me because of the unpleasant attitude exhibited. Sometimes unintentionally, but honestly, most of the time I knew exactly how I was behaving. Being *cold,* you know there's another term I can use, had become so easy. I could turn it on at a moment's notice, and most often for no reason at all.

If I was in a mood, everyone around me knew it; they felt it. My significant other wasn't for it though; he suggested that I do something about it. I could've snapped on him, truth is I probably did, but unfortunately, he was right. I think it hit home when my sister told me that her fiancé didn't want to participate in group dates anymore because of how uncomfortable I made everyone feel when I was in one of my funks. I remember that night like it was yesterday. Everything I held inside was being thrown at the people I care about. Some of the hurt, disappointment, and rejection I'd experienced was caused by my actions. Being a counselor, I recognized that this problem was something I couldn't handle alone. I needed help. I couldn't continue carrying all that negative weight around, and I surely couldn't continue allowing my hurt to hurt other people. I'd always say *every counselor needs a counselor*, and it was time I followed my own philosophy. I found a counselor and that's when the real work began.

I was eight years into my grief, and during those eight years I merely existed; at times, barely existing. Everything on the inside of me was gone, pronounced *dead*, and until that point, I wasn't trying to revive it. I had more important things on my life's agenda, things like trying to figure out how to get a family of my own. I thought if I could find the right man to marry, I could have another baby. Not that I was trying to replace Jayden, because that could never happen, but I wanted a do-over; I wanted my opportunity to bring a healthy baby home.

For me to have the husband and family I desired, I needed to fix me. The broken me was breaking every possible relationship, and that had to change. So, I laid it out, I sat before my counselor, presented all my baggage and instructed her to fix me. Now, being a counselor, I knew *she* couldn't fix me, that task was all mine, but the anointing on this lady's life was so strong, I was certain she'd be able to help me. And help me, she did.

The mask I wore made my outside look somewhat appealing, but if you were able to take a peek at the inside, you might find yourself gagging a little. The process wasn't easy. There were layers of hurt and pain that had to be peeled away until we finally made it to the source; the real sore. The wound that was still infected and causing other parts of me to decay. Before seeking help, I felt I'd earned the right to be sad and angry. I wore my hurt like a badge and couldn't comprehend why others were pressuring me to get rid of it. I'd earned the right to be unhappy. To be miserable. No one should have to hold their baby in a small box on their lap, kiss him, and leave him in the ground. Answer this for me, what did I have to be happy about?

After several therapy sessions, she gave me my final assignment.

"I want you to write Jayden a letter telling him goodbye, releasing him. You have to write it and bring it back to your next session."

I thought, *it's been eight years and I haven't released him, what makes her think I'm doing that now? Okay, I have to write this letter, but not today.* When it comes to therapy, I take it seriously. I believe in the whole process. If I believe it'll work for my clients, shouldn't I believe it would work for me? I sat down several times to type a letter to my deceased son, but I couldn't; I didn't want to say goodbye, I didn't even want to say see you later. Yes, eight years, almost nine, I was still selfish, and I was still angry. And I felt justified in it all.

My next appointment happened to fall on Jayden's ninth birthday. I didn't realize it at the time. I asked her to schedule me in two weeks as she normally did. It was days before the appointment, and I still hadn't written the letter. Since I knew it was coming, it was time for me to make myself. I prayed, opened my computer, and began to write.

October 2014

Dear Jayden,

I was instructed to write you a letter as a way to finally say goodbye or emotionally release you. Honestly, I don't want to do this and have waited almost until the last minute to put my thoughts on a document. Although I don't want to own that you are gone, I really don't want to say it, and I don't want to say goodbye, but I feel like it is finally time for me to do it. I feel like you'll be ok with it. For years I never wanted you to think that I forgot about you. So, I'd make sure to grieve by being sad, crying, withdrawing, finding a way to honor you, acknowledging your life (although it was short), just any way I could celebrate and remember you.

When I found out I was pregnant, I was afraid and super excited at the same time. Probably more afraid though. I didn't know what would happen with my life, but I *did* know that I wanted to do all that I could to afford you the best life possible. I was determined to finish school and start work. Your dad is a good guy; he's just misguided. He had his priorities jacked up. He did illegal things, and although he was happy you were coming, I'm not sure of how great of a dad he would have been with the lifestyle he chose to live. But deep down inside I thought that you might change his life. I thought that you might be the reason he did some things differently. I figured your life would've saved your dad and would possibly seal what he and I shared. I realize now that would've been so much pressure for such a little life; that wasn't your responsibility.

Jayden there is so much I could say to prolong releasing you, but I'm going to be obedient. What I will say is that you have made the greatest impact on my life. I think that you impacted others' lives as well, but you made the greatest impact on your mother. You taught me a deeper love, sacrifice, endurance, survival, and faith. With you I felt love, happiness, joy, hurt, pain, anger, fear, guilt, numbness, loneliness, bitterness, and disgust.

I wanted so badly to be selfish and keep you for myself and my purposes, I didn't want God to take my child. I never understood why He had to use you. Why I had to suffer for you to fulfill your purpose. Some of the questions I have I'll never be able to answer, some of the feelings I experienced I'll never understand, some of the hurt may never end, but I can't hold you here anymore. I can't be selfish or disobedient any longer. I can't have my way. I have to allow you to be with Jesus. I have learned that His ways are not our ways, and if I never understood that, I certainly learned that with you. If it were up to me, you'd still be here, nine years old today. I wouldn't be releasing you; I'd be throwing you a party, giving you gifts, making you feel awfully special. If I had my way we'd be spending today together, but because my ways are not His ways I have celebrated you differently every year.

Some years I've cried, some years I've been quiet, some years people remembered, and they checked on me, some years they didn't. What I have learned to accept is that God knew. He knew I'd hurt, He knew there would be suffering, He knew that I wouldn't want to let go, but He knew I'd survive. And I have. It's been hard, you've been missed, it's been sad and depressing, but it's presented me with growth. It's pushed me into the Kisha I'm supposed to be. It's been a journey that I'll never forget.

For nine years there's been a hole in my heart that I have allowed to stay wounded and open. I've picked at it and reopened the sore sometimes, but I'm finally ready to allow that wound to be healed. Writing you this I'm experiencing body pains, in my back, my chest; tears fall down my face, I want to scream, and honestly, I still don't know if this will happen. Will I allow myself to be made whole again? For this long I've lived with this hurt; *why let it go now?* I sometimes think. But I do want to be better, I do want to not hurt, and not forget you, but I do want to move forward. When I think of you I don't want to cry; I want to smile, I want to be happy. I want to have enough faith to know that God will restore my heart, provide me with answers, and even if I don't get answers I'll have to be okay with that, and move forward with life.

Jayden Charles Wallace, your mother misses you more than anything, and honestly, if I could trade my life to have you back, I would. The reality is that's not possible. So today as I wish you a happy ninth birthday I release you back to heaven with Jesus. I recognize God called you for a particular purpose, and once your purpose was fulfilled, He called you back home. I recognize that sometimes we don't always get what we want, and we have to live with that. And I've learned that if we hold on to hurt and the past we will never enjoy the present and the future. I have chosen to carry you emotionally for nine years, but today I choose to release you. I choose to not burden myself with carrying a loss, not making myself feel sad or hold on to what's not anymore, not make you feel responsible, and not use your short life as a reason for me to be stuck.

Today Jayden, I recognize that God knows what's best for me now and knew what was best for you November 2, 2005 when He called you home. Today I claim wholeness, healing, restoration, peace, joy, happiness and forward progress. I thank God for you and your life, but I won't hurt any longer because of it or allow it to be my excuse. Today I choose to be healed from the hurt of your premature death, and I choose to live for today and no longer my past. Know that I will miss you and I will always love you, and I most definitely won't forget you. But to remember you I don't have to hold on to this hurt. Today, I commit to allowing God to complete the work so that I don't have to carry this hurt any longer. Jayden, I love you, and for your ninth birthday, I release you back to God, your Father.

Love always,
Mommy

Writing that letter was almost as hard as saying *"yes, remove him from the ventilator."* It was just as hard as answering questions to plan a five-day-old baby's funeral. It was just as hard as the funeral director walking the white box to me and sitting it on my lap. Just as hard as having the many guests walk by to view his body and pay their last respects. Just as hard as my final chance to hold him, to look at him, and to kiss him. One final moment with my son, my cheerleader, my angel. Writing that letter didn't make it any easier, but it did begin the process to wholeness--something I never thought I'd have again. The assignment was finally complete.

The night before my session I woke up at about 4 A.M in so much pain. A pain that was almost unbearable. Before going to bed, I felt fine. I had no idea where the piercing pain came from or why it was happening, all I knew was that I couldn't be sick because I had to make it to a session at 9 A.M. so I could release Jayden. I'd made my way to the bathroom, scrunched over in a ball of pain.

I said, *"devil, I will not be sick. I will make it to the session. I have to make it to the session."* I prayed and asked God to remove the pain. After a while, I finally made it back to my bed and attempted to go back to sleep. A few hours later when the alarm sounded, I woke up sore, tired, and drained, but despite how I was feeling, I was determined to make it to my session. It was Jayden's ninth birthday, and the day I would be free, *I hoped.*

"Did you complete your assignment?' My counselor asked.

I pulled the letter from my purse, but before reading, I told her about my experience earlier that morning. I told her how the devil tried to prevent me from coming that day, but as I started to explain, something dawned on me, and I couldn't speak. I was finally processing what happened that morning, and it wasn't the devil after all. Sometimes we give him much more credit than he deserves. The same time I was in the bathroom that morning was around the same time I delivered Jayden the exact same date, nine years prior. As I began to figure it out, my therapist looked and said the words I'll never forget.

"God purged you," she stated without hesitation.

I realized I was giving the devil credit for God's work. God allowed me to *birth* Jayden all over again, not physically but spiritually and emotionally, so that I could release him. (This is what I meant when I talked about giving birth a second time). I know it sounds weird, but I know that's what happened and after that, I felt free.

I removed my letter from the envelope and began to read. As I read, something very different happened from all the other times, even from now. I didn't shed a lot of tears, and that peace I'd experienced in the Neonatal Intensive Care Unit with Jayden, I was feeling again. I read the letter, releasing my 9 year- old to his Father, which in turn released the tight grip pain had on me.

When I finished reading, I looked up and asked, "Do you think this is going to work?"

"If you want it to" Was her simple, yet powerful response.

I not only wanted it to, but I needed it to.

Releasing Jayden a second time was just as hard as the first, but it had to happen so God could demonstrate His healing power to me and those around me. Yes, there are days I still cry and miss him. Usually, his birthday is hard. I still have my moments on Mother's Day and holidays, but even those days don't have the same hold on me anymore. I once felt trapped in pain with no room to wiggle my way out. Years ago, I couldn't see all the promises and purpose that were in that pain; I had blinders on that only allowed me to see pain.

What I've learned through this experience is that most often when we're in pain it's not due to one thing, but several things that are built up and cause us to feel that we aren't strong enough to endure. When I think about it, pain is like an onion. It comes with layers; it stinks, burns your eyes, and tends to make you cry. When you're cutting an onion, the goal is to get it done as quickly as possible. Isn't that how we are with pain?

What if I told you pain is packed with purpose? What if I told you on the other side of pain is something great enough to make the pain worth enduring? Would that make you want to take your time to *dice the onion?* Maybe not. Or perhaps you'd tough through what feels agonizing just to see what awaits you on the other side of pain. I'm not completely there yet, but I'm much further along than I was before writing and reading that letter to release my baby boy. I promise there's beauty on the other side of pain. There's joy on the other side of pain. There's relief on the other side of pain. When we work through it, He rewards you for your endurance with a gift that makes the pain worthwhile. He then reveals purpose in pain.

Let me encourage you in the midst of your pain. You need to know that you're not alone. There are many little girls hurting! You must remain in the fight. You have no idea who's watching. Who's being encouraged by your endurance. Some only have the strength to stand because you didn't give up. You're stronger than you think, Sis! So much stronger! When you arise, you'll forget about the pain and embrace the purpose. I know that you may be nursing your pain right now, and while you are be reminded that pain has a purpose; allow God to breathe life in your painful and *dead* situations now because little girl, it is time, arise.

## Prayer

Lord,

I don't want to stop doing what You've called me to do just because sometimes it hurts. I ask in moments that are unbearable, and the pain becomes intolerable that You bring to my remembrance the purpose in that pain. Give me a glimpse of what's on the other side of pain. I'm asking that You use pain to produce purpose in my life. Lord, pain is what knocked me down, pain is what's trying to take me out, but if I see pain from Your perspective, I'd see that there's a reward so great on the other side of pain, strength is developed through pain, and growth is a result of pain. You demonstrated the benefit of pain when Jesus went to the cross and died for me. I know that was a painful situation to endure, but You endured, and because You endured I have access to abundant life. I will not allow pain to paralyze me nor cause me to fear or abort the birthing process that I am in. Give this *little girl* the tenacity to push through the pain and help me endure until I'm on the other side and able to birth the purpose You created me for. Lord, You know I'm not good with pain, and I don't want to hurt, but I know that there is a reason for this painful experience, and I embrace it because I now know the greatness that You'll bring forth from my pain. In Jesus Name. Amen.

# Chapter 4:
## Purpose

"Tarkisha you know there may be times when you may feel as if you're not helping people. But you're so special and God placed you here on PURPOSE. You're farrrrr from perfect (we all are), you may have picked up some ways along the way...but watch the shift that's about to take place with you. Don't be surprised if people fall off that you wouldn't have imagined would. But you will be surrounded by people who love you for TARKISHA, flaws and all!! Not just for your money because these people don't care about that. God is doing something. Jesus The Christ!"

After years of growing through my pain, I finally came to a point in my life where I needed to know my purpose; I mean we all have one...right? All I had to do was figure mine out, and that's just what I set out to do! I set out to discover my purpose. I had it all planned out for myself; however, it hadn't seemed to quite work out my way. While I was working so hard at *my* purpose for my life, *yes, my purpose*, my plans kept failing.

I realized other things were coming to me, but not the things I desperately desired. I found myself getting frustrated and making comments like *"God, I didn't ask you for any of this! All I asked of You was to let me have my own family. And You keep giving me everything except that!"* I have a great job, which has helped me grow professionally and has afforded me opportunities I thought would take years to obtain. I started my own business and had a beautiful home; I had everything that most people long for, but I had no one to share it with. And while I should've been joyous, which a part of me was, there was another part that felt nothing but sadness. I didn't want God to think I was ungrateful and take everything away, so I always expressed my gratitude. I couldn't say thank you enough, but I still couldn't help thinking how that wasn't the life I'd envisioned. Eventually, I had to choose to either continue looking at the lack or start looking at the gain. I decided to focus on what I *did* have, and all the blessings that continued to flow even when I thought I had more than enough. I was finally able to recognize the favor of God on my life. Finally, I learned to be content with His plans, even though they were different than my own.

I don't know about you, but I'm so glad God loves me enough to say no. Isn't it amazing how God's plans for our lives are always far better than what we could've pieced together? It validates Jeremiah 29:11 for me. *"For I know the plans I have for you! Plans to prosper you."* He knew that His plans, if I were patient enough to wait for it, would bring me what I wanted, and things I never imagined I would have.

Who knew He'd take my pain and passion, and use them to thrust me into my purpose? *My true purpose.* The purpose He had for me. The whole reason I was created in the first place.

Who knew God would use, little ole me*?* This little girl who died in November 2005, the same little girl that oozed death on everything she encountered thereafter. The one who had no plans of getting over the hurt she experienced, and most definitely no plans on telling anyone that experienced the same or similar hurt that they'd be able to make it through. It's hard to sell people a promise that even you don't believe yourself. I began to realize why the revelation of my purpose was delayed. God had to make sure I was ready.

Had I known that the road leading to my purpose included a deep, dark valley, and in this valley, I'd carry a baby, birth him, and bury him soon after...had God stopped by my apartment, sat on my couch, and gave me the details of His plan, I'm sure my response would've been similar to yours: *"Nah God, I'm good. Use someone else for this one. I'm not your girl."*

It was in my valley experience where God went to work in my life. On the outside, I looked well put together, but my inside was disgusting. God had to create in me the woman He needed me to be; He couldn't send the little girl that cried more than she smiled, and who frequently threw parties where pity was the only invited guest. In my valley, He had to break me so that He could mend me. He had to allow some things to hurt me so that He could restore me. He allowed some things to die so that the things He birthed through me would get the nurturing and attention it required. God had to go through what I consider extreme measures, so He could use me.

[25]

I've often heard if you're praying for patience or to be used, then be prepared because to receive patience, you have to endure situations that will test and strengthen your patience. For God to use you at your full potential, you have to prove that your faith and your trust are strong enough to withstand your circumstances. He's never going to put us in a position to be used without proper preparation; and if you're unaware, let me be the first to enlighten you, preparation hurts…. a lot.

To be completely transparent, there are many times I consider had I truly known all I would encounter; I would've never asked to be used. I would've settled for safe and remained quiet and content in my comfort zone. That life was easy. It didn't feel like I was on a consistent rollercoaster, with challenges, tragedy, adversity, and disappointment. Had I known what was waiting on the other side of that prayer request, I probably would've chosen a life I've seen on TV or in the movies or one like the fairytales I used to read as a child. Or maybe I would've chosen someone's life I actually know. A life that looks well put together and *troublefree*. But then I remembered the lyrics to a song by Jonathan McReynolds that says, "you spend all night admiring pictures, they make life look perfect, as they should. But you don't know the picture's story, and how long it took to make it good." He was exactly right. The main thing we must remember is there's purpose in each of our journeys, and we have to experience every aspect of the journey the way God intends, if we are going to fully operate in our purpose.

Had you asked me to define my purpose when I was around eleven years-old, I would've answered without hesitation, *"Simple. By the time I'm twenty-one I'll be married and starting a family."* That was all I knew for sure. Each year I added a little more to the life I dreamed for myself. Work wasn't my biggest concern. Being rich or wealthy didn't matter a whole lot either. I didn't care about seeing the world, and I'm more than positive I wasn't thinking about using my life to help others. All I knew was once I finished high school, I would go to college and meet a man who would become my husband and the father of my children. A man who'd take good care of us, and we'd live happily ever after. You know, the simple life. At that time, I had one goal, getting to college and my purpose would then be fulfilled. At least that's what I thought; little girls, I was completely wrong.

As I reflect over my life, I've acknowledged that between the dates of October 29, 2005, through November 2, 2005, when my child's life began and ended, I was being positioned for purpose. Jayden accomplished his purpose, and God was positioning his mommy to fulfill hers. I didn't know then how God would use it, and to be honest, I wasn't interested in knowing and neither did I care. I was selfish and wanted what was mine. But it was me that asked to be used, and if my purpose was going to be fulfilled, I had to have the full experience, not just the glamorous ending. While I was trying to make my fairytale come true, God was preparing me to survive a nightmare that would one day be my ministry. He knew what He put inside of me, and exactly what had to happen to bring it out of me.

I've asked God numerous times, "Why me? Why my baby? Why did you allow this to happen to me? Why 'use' me this way?" Here's what I concluded: God knew that He could trust me with the assignment. Once I'm dedicated to something, I'm all in. I pursue it passionately because, for me, it's another step toward healing, not only for me but also for those connected to me. God knew He needed to show me that I could survive the darkest hours of my life. Through me, He's now able to demonstrate His strength to others. He also knew I'd never take the credit for His work. I understand that I survived only because of Him, and that's the message I never fail to share with others.

I'm finally aligned with God's plan. He chose me and now instead of feeling bitter and hurt, I feel honored, but most of all, humbled. That dying moment in my life happened and affected me the way that it did so that someone can see my recovery, my survival, my triumph, my strength, and use that as the needed encouragement to resuscitate what died in her. It happened so that one day another little girl would arise!

## *Prayer*

God, I know that You have a purpose for my life. Help me to recognize and embrace Your purpose for me, the reason You created me. Help me to part ways with my plan and align with what You've designed. Father, I'm not fond of pain or suffering, I don't want to have days of sadness or loneliness. On a daily basis, I want to experience joy, but I understand that there will be situations in my life that test my strength, endurance, integrity, and faithfulness, all in preparation for purpose. Help me to maintain joy and smile through those tough times just as I smile through the good. I also ask for peace for the moments when I'm not satisfied or content. Lord, it's in those moments I pray You'll surround me with Your perfect peace. I ask that Your will and purpose for my life supersede any other plans or dreams that others or myself may have for me. I want You to be able to trust me with the assignment. When my faith is tested, when I want to fold, when I want out because I think I can't take it anymore, send a reminder of who I am in You, exercise Your strength through me, and help me remember that suffering lasts only for a period of time. I ask that You strengthen me to face whatever comes along with Your purpose for my life and that You equip me with integrity, so I'll never jeopardize or compromise who I am when things get difficult. I know that what You bring to me, You've prepared me to get through. So, when purpose doesn't seem like the most fun or easiest thing to engage in, send Your Holy Spirit to push me until I'm where You've destined me to be. Thank You for my life's purpose, thank you for seeing fit to use me. In Jesus Name. Amen.

## *Workbook Reminder:*

Complete the activities in your *Little Girl Arise* Workbook about *purpose*. If you are unaware of your purpose, not fully walking in your purpose, or have been waiting to give your all to your purpose, the time is now. Someone else's purpose is dependent on you fulfilling yours. There's a little girl waiting to arise, but you must fulfill your purpose for her to do so.

# Little Girl Arise

## Chapter 5:

### Forgiveness

Forgiveness isn't easy. For some, it's one of the hardest things to do. I've learned that forgiveness isn't a task; instead, it's a process. First, the action or words that hurt us replay in our mind. Then, even if an apology is offered, it's hard to accept immediately because we need to know that they've learned their lesson and paid for their actions. For some, forgiveness can only come after vengeance. And for many, it's not forgiving that's the challenge, it's forgetting.

I believe this chapter is where God is going to begin the good *work* in you that He has been waiting to complete. This is the chapter where you may find yourself saying, "wow, all it took was forgiveness?" As I prayed before beginning this chapter, God reminded me of a few words from The Lord's Prayer; "and forgive us our trespasses, as we forgive those who trespass against us." He spoke clearly to me, "you often want My forgiveness, and I want to extend it to you, but you must forgive those that have done the unforgivable to you." To arise, we must let go and forgive.

Sometimes it's hard to feel things while you're going through it. You may not feel the weight of unforgiveness, how it holds you down and prevents you from progressing. However, forgiveness is freeing. Unforgiveness keeps you stuck in neutral, or even worse, causes you to go in reverse. How can we truly press forward if we're still mentally stuck reliving every detail of our past hurt? We are so concerned with the "trespasser's" role in forgiveness that we fail to do our part.

I have learned forgiveness is two-sided; there's extending forgiveness and receiving forgiveness. You may think you only have control of one side, which is the extending side; however, you have some control of both sides. How so? There's an old saying that says, "You may have to accept the apology you never get." That's where our control lies when we are offended. There may be times you're going to have to say, "I forgive you," without an apology being offered. You'll have to release them and let go of the pain that others may have caused without them ever acknowledging, owning, or being accountable for their actions.

Trust me, I know that's challenging. We live in a time where apologies are expected. If someone wronged us, they'd need to admit it, apologize, and go to the end of the earth, in word and deed, to show us they're truly sorry. Am I right when I say we expect others to apologize and prove that they're worthy of being forgiven? This means we've forgiven them, conditionally. And if those conditions aren't met to our standards, then we immediately revoke the acceptance and move backward to unforgiveness.

Eventually, we all must learn that letting go is for our own good. Not only letting go of the pain, but sometimes there will be people that we're going to have to let go of. There are going to be moments that we sit with ourselves, silence the noise, nurse our wounds, and forgive the person that never says, "I was wrong, I hurt you. I'm sorry for treating you in such a way. I'm sorry for neglecting you. I am sorry for rejecting you. I'm sorry for betraying you. I'm sorry for leaving you when you needed me the most. I'm sorry for saying one thing but doing another. I'm sorry for always prioritizing my needs over yours. I'm sorry for not supporting you. I'm sorry for being selfish. I'm sorry for devaluing you, never acknowledging and honoring your worth. I'm sorry for taking advantage of you. I'm sorry for having motives that would benefit me more than you. I'm sorry for not being who you needed me to be when I knew I couldn't be that person to or for you. I'm sorry for not loving you the way you should've been loved, the way you needed to be loved, the way that you deserved to be loved." One of the most difficult challenges we may face in life is saying *I forgive you* to the person who hasn't admitted their fault.

I'd like you to take a moment for reflection. I must warn you, it won't feel good, but hopefully, it'll open your eyes. I challenge you to sit and reflect on a time you intentionally said something hurtful to or sabotaged someone, the time you lied to someone, cheated on them, or betrayed them. Take some time to think about when you were not the most dependable or committed person, the loyal friend, devoted significant other, ideal wife, *employee of the month* type of employee, or those times you weren't the ideal Christian.

The point of this reflection isn't to evoke guilt for the not so nice ways you may have treated others, but for you to recognize, although you've been hurt, you're not perfect and at some point, in the past, and possibly in the future, you have and may possibly hurt others also. During these times you'll need to be forgiven, and just like you'd want them to readily forgive you, you should be open and ready to forgive others.

When it comes to forgiveness there are two things I hear a lot, *"forgive and forget"* and *"hurt people, hurt people."* I'm sure you've heard these before as well. As a counselor, I can say that I haven't witnessed too many people who were actually able to forgive AND forget. And all too often, I've seen hurting people who have the tendency of hurting others; even those who were trying to help them heal. I wish I could tell you that I know this to be true because of all the research I've conducted, but no, that's not how I know at all. Everything I'm sharing I've learned through experience, counseling with clients, and from the Holy Spirit.

Now, when it comes to forgiving and forgetting, I believe I've finally come to understand the *forgetting* part. Once I realized how replaying the hurt was only causing me to hurt more, I knew I had to make a change, especially if I've already forgiven the person. When I said, *"I accept your apology,"* they believed me. I'd witness them move on with their lives; meanwhile, I remained stuck wasting time in a hurtful past when I should've been focusing on the happier present, and all the possibilities of the future. This lesson was by far one of the hardest to learn, but it was worth it. And once I did, my stress level significantly decreased, and my level of peace went up a notch. I'm not saying that there aren't times I struggle with the *forgetting* part, but I will tell you when I've followed through with forgetting, my life became a little more simplified and a lot less gloomy.

## *Forgiveness: A Spiritual Look*

There are many scriptures in the Bible, which teach forgiveness, and gospel artist, Helen Baylor, sang a song, Sea of Forgetfulness, which demonstrates what *forgive and forget* means. I've shared a few of the many scriptures regarding forgiveness, and I strongly encourage you to take some time to truly digest the scriptures. Meditate on each one. I pray that through these scriptures you'll find a greater understanding of forgiving then forgetting.

- Micah 7: 19 (The Message Bible) – "And compassion is on its way to us. You'll stamp out our wrongdoing. You'll sink our sins to the bottom of the ocean."
- Hebrews 8:12 (The Message Bible) – "They'll get to know me by being kindly forgiven, with the slate of their sins forever wiped clean."
- Isaiah 43:25 (The Message Bible) – "But I, yes I, am the one who takes care of your sins-- that's what I do. I don't keep a list of your sins."

Considering these scriptures and the song, Sea of Forgetfulness, my interpretation of *forgiving and forgetting* is this. When someone wrongs me, I should sincerely accept their extension of forgiveness then wipe my memory clean of that *transgression*. Isn't that exactly what God does for us? When we genuinely repent for our sin, He offers us forgiveness, grace, and a clean slate; the Bible tells us *He removes it from His memory*.

While working with a client, who, let's just say, had a *colorful* past, I concluded that forgiveness might've been what he needed in order to make the desired progress. He had difficulty forgiving others and asking for forgiveness. He didn't want an apology; he wanted people to pay for what they did. He didn't offer apologies because he said if he did something he meant to do it, and there was no need in being sorry for it later.

During his sessions, he'd been speaking about things he'd done in his past, which he wasn't proud of. One session he battled with the thought of facing karma because of all his wrongdoing. After probing and processing for a while I asked him, "What about forgiveness? If you ask for forgiveness from the people you've done these things to, and God, then you may receive grace. Karma can't penetrate grace." He immediately informed me that there were some things he absolutely couldn't admit to doing. If he would have, he'd possibly put himself in the position to receive very serious consequences. Therefore, in his mind, since he couldn't admit these things and apologize to those he wronged, he felt like he couldn't truly be forgiven.

After several sessions of getting the story out, I introduced forgiveness; it was with this client I explored what it means to *forgive and forget*. After presenting the concept to him, his response was quite interesting. He said, "oh no, I'm not going to forget, and I'm going to make sure the person remembers what they did so they don't cross me again." This client believed in payback. He wanted revenge, and you better believe he was going to get it. He viewed accepting forgiveness as allowing the person to get away with whatever they did, and he was not okay with that.

The client challenged me on forgetting, "How am I supposed to forget? Why should I forget? And if I do forget, then they'll think they can do it again."

I pondered for a moment before responding. "You're right. It's hard to forgive and forget. Some people will take advantage of that and may hurt you again. Some people abuse forgiveness and expect it each time they wrong you. So yes, I get it, it's hard to forget when a person is a repeat offender."

He nodded his head in agreement, but I wasn't done. "But," I continued, "a person that abuses your forgiveness or takes it for granted is telling you, through their actions, that you have to change your interactions with them. By doing so, you remove their opportunity to repeatedly harm you. I get it; the bottom line is you have to protect yourself."

In no way am I suggesting that we are to repeatedly allow people to mistreat, disrespect, or misuse us; I'm saying, if they do, forgive them...for your own sake. We are in control of whom we allow in our lives. If there is a person that hurts us and apologizes only to do it again and again, then that person may be someone we take time to consider the necessity of their connection. We shouldn't ever allow others to intentionally hurt us, repeatedly. We have to put a stop to it but are still expected to extend and accept forgiveness.

So why do I agree with forgetting? Quite honestly, because the memory of the hurt is sometimes as painful as the moment it happened. As you all have read, I don't like pain, and I try to avoid it at all cost. Remembering everything that people who offended me did has the potential to cause me to relive those unpleasant moments. First, the memories resurface than the hurt returns followed by scrambled emotions, and all of a sudden, I'm hurting again from things that happened years ago. Things that I'd accepted apologies for, but seemingly had never truly forgiven and certainly hadn't forgotten.

Choosing to not forget is choosing to hold on to the pain. If we're to be more like Christ, we have to forgive and forget those wrongdoings, "sink them into the bottom of the ocean." Visualize that for a moment. Picture yourself tying weights to those hurtful memories then physically throwing them into the ocean and watching them sink. Now, see yourself diving in after it. Does that look like a pretty picture to you? Would you risk your health, peace, and happiness to retrieve those memories?

When I *finally* chose to forgive and forget, I found myself at a place of peace. I wasn't toying with why they did it or wondering if they would do it again. For my sanity, I had to choose forgiveness; otherwise, my offender would maintain too much control when they shouldn't have had any at all. I'm still growing in this area; I'm still tested, but I have decided that I will choose forgiveness!

# Little Girl Arise
## Forgiveness: Do the Work

So often we hear the saying, "hurt people, hurt people." Though it's quite unfortunate, it's the truth. However, I don't believe this is the motive of the hurting person. I think that the intentions start off pure, but the poison from past hurts seep out onto those we love and those trying to love us. Isn't it crazy that the people we tend to hurt are those we love the most? Here's what we do, push those who want to help us away, choosing to remain in a miserable place, alone.

Everything I'm sharing are things I've experienced in life; some I'm currently experiencing. God uses these moments to grow my understanding, increase my wisdom, lengthen my endurance, and demonstrate the dynamic power of forgiveness. If He is to use me to help little girls arise, He has to ensure I understand and live a life of forgiveness.

During the time I chose to live in my pain, I hurt many people who were trying to love me. A guy once told me, "you sabotage your relationships so that you don't get hurt." He was right. Not that I was trying to sabotage the relationships, but I was trying to avoid what I expected. Being hurt in relationships had become a norm for me. It had happened several times before, so I thought why not prepare for the blow.

My best friend would always tell me, "Kisha, you cannot avoid hurt. If a person is going to hurt you, you won't be able to stop them. If you keep thinking everyone is going to hurt you and acting off that thought, you're going to end up losing a lot of good people. Think about it. Not everyone is out to get or hurt you." She continued, "And Kisha, if they do hurt you, you'll make it. You're strong."

She was right, but for some reason, I was always prepared to respond to their hurt or hurt them before they had the opportunity to hurt me. My philosophy was if you hurt me, I'd hurt you worse, but my goal was to determine if they were going to hurt me and try to block the blow. However, if a person was successful at hurting me, when retaliating, I made sure when I struck they felt it, remembered it, and thought twice before hurting me again. The downside was I pushed people away because I was too busy anticipating the moment they'd let me down.

I packed my bag of hurt from previous relationships and carried it right on over into the relationship that followed. It became a cycle. In my mind I needed that bag; carrying it allowed me to open it up as needed and reflect on everything that was done to me, and if I saw a hint of any of those actions in my new relationship, I knew exactly what to do. Get them before they got me. That hurt little girl leaked her venom on and sabotaged many relationships, friendships, and connections, when all I had to do was accept the apology that was never extended, take it for what it was, learn a lesson, and release it. Nope, not me. But I didn't know any better; I was a little girl.

It was when my most promising relationship failed that I finally learned I had to take time and deal with me. Particularly, I needed to evaluate the hurt I was carrying. It was necessary to think about everything that had ever hurt me then assess the damage holding on to it was causing. After that period of reflection, I knew I had to do something. I realized my way wasn't working, and I had to admit to myself it wasn't going to be any different until I decided to make a change. In case you're wondering how I did it, the answer is quite simple. When I went to counseling, learning and practicing forgiveness was a part of the work.

Around the time I started processing and working on me, one evening my friend invited me to join a prayer call. As the speaker spoke and prayed, I was immediately intrigued; I was fully attentive. I remember her saying the spiritual seasons were about to change in our lives, but to move into our next season, we had to forgive. She said God wouldn't be able to advance us if we didn't practice forgiveness.

When disconnecting from the call I knew one thing, I couldn't be left behind; I wanted to get to my next season. So, I started writing what came to be a very long list of people I owed an apology and those I needed to forgive. That list was an eye-opener. I thought, *wow, I did all this to this many people?* That very night, it was well after 11 P.M., but I couldn't allow another minute to pass, I started calling, texting and emailing those I'd hurt and those who hurt me. I asked for forgiveness and finally forgave those who hurt me. I even forgave people who never offered an apology. At one point, my flesh attempted to overrule my spirit by trying to convince me it wasn't a good idea to forgive one person. *It'll open a door for them to re-engage you*, I heard my flesh saying. I managed to push pride aside and sent that one last email.

My mom is like my spiritual mentor, so I share a lot of my spiritual encounters with her. Once I finished my assignment of asking for and accepting forgiveness, I told my mom about the exercise. And just like a mother, she said, "Now Kisha, don't go making another list." In mom language that meant, "You've cleared this list. Don't fill it up again. Don't hurt anyone else." I've done my best to avoid hurting others, and if by chance I do, I immediately try to make it right.

Speaking of my mom, you may not believe it, but she was someone on my list. After losing my son, a lot of my mental and emotional anger was directed at her. She'd done nothing wrong but isn't it like us to always find someone to blame. Since she was the one who told me, "Send Jayden back to God the way He sent him to you. It's time," I was angry with her. She never knew it, and I probably would've never told her had I not decided to write this book. The purpose of sharing it now is to show the importance of self-evaluation. It was afterward that I realized my anger was misplaced, and that to heal I had to recognize it, deal with it, and ask for forgiveness.

I'm well aware that forgiving isn't the easiest thing to do, but once you forgive you'll be happier, better, braver, and you'll be stronger than you've ever been in your life. I'm not only encouraging you, these are facts! If I can go through and overcome life obstacles, I am quite confident each of you can as well. However, like me, you must be willing to start with forgiveness. Forgive others, repent to God, and allow Him to work on you. This will lead to the wholeness and healing you desire.

## *Forgiveness Includes You*

The most important extension of forgiveness we'll ever give will be to ourselves. Sometimes we give ourselves such a hard time for bad decisions we've made. We mentally and emotionally abuse ourselves, all because we won't forgive ourselves. Think about it, if you can forgive and request forgiveness from others, what good is that if you're holding yourself hostage for your transgressions?

Why torture yourself by reminiscing about the mistakes you've made or the hurt you've felt? Why toss and turn during the night trying to figure out why this happened or what you did to deserve it? Why question every motive, every action, and every word that burned you? If you've truly forgiven and have been forgiven, what sense does it make to allow your mind to keep you stuck in pain? In turmoil? In guilt? As a victim? Why?

It's time that you understand your value and worth; you're worth your forgiveness. The next time you disappoint yourself, miss the target, or just completely fall off, extend yourself that same forgiving grace that you'd offered to others. Forgiving others is important, but total peace comes once you forgive yourself.

Unforgiveness is an unnecessary weight. It's not going to help you in any way. It's not going to ease any pain. It's not going to get anyone back. It's not going to make you feel better. Unforgiveness will destroy you. It will ruin every relationship, opportunity, goal, or mission you encounter because you're stuck waiting for it to go wrong because that's what happened before.

At different points of life, I was angry with several people and refused to forgive them. I felt all those individuals were going on with their lives as if they'd never hurt me. They were moving forward, and I was left in the same place bitter and angry. *How could they continue as if they hadn't ruined my life?* Not forgiving them and not forgiving myself deepened the pain, but when I realized the benefit in releasing and pardoning them and forgiving myself my life changed. I began to heal.

Little girl, if you and I are going to arise, we cannot be weighed down. Release the weight and lessen the pressure.

Forgive, it's for your own sake.

# Little Girl Arise

## Prayer

Father God,

Forgiving others is not easy at all; sometimes forgiving myself is even more difficult. Help me to follow Your example of forgiveness and forgive others as You've instructed me to. If someone offends me, You said I should forgive them seventy times seven times, and when I forgive them, I should remember it no more. I want to be more like You in that area of my life. I want to practice forgiveness, walk-in forgiveness, and live a forgiving life. Lord, even more so, I want to avoid doing things that hurt people and require them to forgive me. Help me change my ways so that I discontinue hurting or disappointing others. Help me to be mindful of my words and actions. Help me to be sensitive to the needs and feelings of others. I ask that You help me avoid operating from a revenge mentality, but from a place of forgiveness. I know that I cannot *arise* if I'm weighed down. I thank You that as I begin to forgive others, letting go of what they have done to offend me, and allow You to take care of it, I will arise to fulfill the purpose You have for my life. In Jesus Name. Amen.

## Workbook Reminder

*Forgiveness can be freeing. It can be the release we have desired, and the key to our next level. How can we truly press forward if we're still mentally parked in what and who hurt us, how they hurt us, why they hurt us, and wondering why they won't own their actions and try to make amends.* Don't forget to complete the activities in your *Little Girl Arise* Workbook based on *forgiveness*. If we start here and follow through, half the battle is complete.

# Chapter 6:
## Faith and Wisdom

Without wisdom, we will mess up what faith produces.

Have you ever wanted something so bad, you begged God for it? You worry Him like none other, asking for that desire. In your world, nothing is more important at that time. I know this feeling all too well. There have been times when He's provided immediately, but there were more times where He's made me wait.

It's in these waiting periods when I tend to get extremely frustrated. *Why won't God release everything I've asked Him for, right when I ask Him for it?* Sometimes it seems that He picks and chooses what He gives me and when He gives it to me. I can almost hear Him saying,

"Yes, I'll release this for her now," or "This request she needs to wait on," or "I'll give her a sneak peak, but she's not ready for that just yet."

I want to ask, "What do You mean I'm not ready? I'm ready, and I'm ready right now."

Isn't He supposed to give me all the desires of my heart? He said, if I delight myself in Him then He'd give me the desires of my heart (Psalm 37:4). I've heard a person say that we have those desires because God placed them there. Well, He put the desires there, "so *ummm* God, what's the holdup?" Ever find yourself asking Him that?

"It's going to happen sooner than you think." That's the prophecy I received about five years ago. Clearly, my definition of sooner and God's definition are much different, because I'm still waiting. I was thinking it was going to happen within a few months, maybe a year…nope. I haven't given up though. I'll keep waiting until it happens. I have faith that it's coming because I prayed for it and God promised it. He just didn't provide me with an exact ETA.

I've noticed that after I ask God for something, even if He doesn't answer immediately, He does give me a little glimpse of what's to come. For example, I want to have children. At one time I wanted four, that's since changed; two may be pushing it. Anyway, I was constantly praying, "God I want a baby, I want a child. I'm getting older, and you know the risks that come with age, so I need to have a baby soon." I don't just want the baby. I want the baby and a husband. This time I want to do it in order like the nursery rhyme instructs, "first comes love, then comes marriage, then comes baby in the baby carriage." I figured if I do it in order, things might have a better outcome.

So, I begged God for children, and then He gives me, what I feel, is a test to see if I'm ready, and if that's what I really wanted at that time in my life. I believe God always needed to see if I could handle the blessing I desired. The test He gave involved two very interesting, yet challenging subjects: my nephew and niece, Kent and Payton. After a day of babysitting those two, having children of my own would be the furthest thing from my mind. Payton talks loud and nonstop from the time she wakes up until she finally goes to sleep... which is usually very late. Did I mention that I enjoy my rest and quiet time?

Then there's Kent, who's like my best friend. He's the bossy best friend, and I'm the "I just want my best friend to be happy" friend. As an aunt, I'm a pushover, and he's got that figured out. Whatever he says goes, whatever he wants he gets.

Kent and Payton are lots of fun; they're two of my favorite little people, but two hours into babysitting and I'm telling God, "I see why you have me waiting, I'm not ready." I can't handle a few hours of babysitting before I'm going crazy; all that talking, moving, and bossing me around. God, You're right to have me wait.

For me, Kent and Payton are great lessons on waiting. God is allowing me the time I need to figure out if this is what I want, and if the answer is still yes, then the next question is, is it necessary to have it right now. After my tee-tee duties are complete, and those two little beings are back with their parents, I'm all for God's plan. Let me clarify that I understand babysitting and having a baby of my own would be quite different. I know once I have my own, my new life will feel normal. However, my faith tells me that there are still things I need to prepare within myself before God sends the blessing.

Perhaps the example of having children didn't reach you; that may not be your area of waiting. Maybe it's a husband or a significant other, I can relate there as well. It could be a career break; the career move that will set you and your family up for the life you've always imagined. For some, it may be a financial increase. You're working the job you love and can't imagine yourself doing anything else, but you need the numbers in your bank account to look a whole lot better. You want to make the money that matches your drive. For some, it may be a real friend. A friend may sound like a simple request, but having experienced betrayal and disloyalty, a *real* friend may be all that you need to sustain you. Someone you can trust with your secrets.

I don't know anyone who's not waiting for something God has promised or something they've asked Him to provide. As long as there are desires, there will be a time to wait; it could be long, or it could be short, but waiting is something we'll all do at some point in our lives. It's important to maintain faith during this waiting period. And while waiting in faith, seek wisdom to know how to maximize on what God is about to release to you.

Let's talk about faith. We all know what faith is, and at some point, or another we've all had to activate it. There are moments when your faith is at its peak, but then there are other moments when it's as low as the valley. Nevertheless, when we need it, we can gather up that mustard seed size faith (Luke 17:6), which will add a little hope to our expectation. Faith is believing, right? We believe that whatever we are seeking and asking He will do. I have faith that He will heal my ailments. I have faith He will help me secure the job. I have faith He will help me pass the test. I have faith He will financially make a way for me to finish school or start my business. I have faith that He's going to watch over my children while they're away at college. I have faith that He'll do the impossible on my behalf because, for me, it's life or death.

Faith is what keeps us going. When the situation looks like it won't go in our favor, its faith that keeps us in the fight. I'm certain it was my faith that kept me praying those five days my son lived. It was faith and knowing that God had done similar things for other people that made me confident in Him doing the same for me. I'm not talking about God healing people and renewing life only in the Bible, but I've seen Him do it in the lives of people I know.

What happens when the results are different from what our faith led us to believe? Faith said, "God is going to do it," but He didn't. Then what happens? Discouragement? Anger and frustration cause doubt when it's time to have faith again? Those are our normal responses.

I remember telling God, "You said to have faith, and I did but look at what happened. Look how it ended. My son died. I had faith, and faith didn't change my situation."

I've learned that when things don't go the way we believe they should, it's quite natural to put faith down and pick up doubt. Talk about a setback. When things don't happen when you want them to happen, the way you foresee it happening, don't lose hope, don't give up, stay in faith. Have you ever heard that a thing isn't over until it ends well? If it didn't end in your definition of well, maintain faith, it's not over.

Doubt, anger, and frustration are very normal feelings, but the minute we give up and allow them to take over, we set ourselves back and extend our waiting period. Many times, we're being tested to see if we'll believe God even when He's clearly said "no." Will we believe Him when the odds are stacked against us? Will we believe Him when the door is slammed shut, not just closed, but slammed shut in our face? Will we believe Him when the result is death even after we've seen Him heal someone from the same disease? Will we remain in faith or be swayed by what our eyes see and our ears hear?

"Faith is the substance of things hoped for and the evidence of things not seen" (Hebrews 11:1). Faith isn't the eyes of the operation; faith is the heart of the operation. It's the gut feeling that confirms your "know." Faith is your spiritual intuition. Faith goes in blindly with a sense of reassurance knowing that because you asked God, because He promised it, because you believe it, it will be. You don't have to see it because you know God. When we exercise faith, we aren't necessarily supposed to *see*, but we are supposed to *believe*. After all, He's a man that can't, won't, and hasn't lied. Without a doubt, you can trust Him. Faith is everything, we certainly need it, but God wants us to seek and exercise wisdom as well. Faith plus Wisdom, that's a winning combination.

I believe faith without wisdom is a recipe for trouble. Wisdom without faith won't produce good results either. We'll find ourselves afraid to step out and do what we know God has called us to do. Living in fear of what could go wrong instead of focusing on what will go right. Having an even balance between faith and wisdom will help us maintain the hope and belief that what we're seeking from God will come to pass, but at its appointed time, when we're truly ready for it.

Wisdom will teach us how to pursue those desires with knowledge, and not jump on everything as soon as the thought enters our mind. Right now, wisdom is teaching me to wait. It's not easy, but necessary. Financially, I can probably support a child, but the way my nerves, quiet time, and sleep operate, God has been right. I can hear Him saying, "Daughter, I want you to have babies, but let Me help you out with this one. Let Me hold them until I know that you're completely prepared. I'll know when you're ready, and at that time, I'll release them to you."

Without wisdom, we'll mess up what faith produces. There have been times God withheld what I've asked for because I wasn't ready for the responsibility or I wouldn't know what to do with it. Maybe I would've messed it up, maybe I wasn't mature enough, maybe I'd take it for granted, or maybe I'd miss an opportunity to learn and grow from it.

Wisdom, in my opinion, is a combination of book knowledge and street sense. You aren't born with it; it's a process of growth; you must learn it. You gain wisdom from observing, doing, listening, and making mistakes. The Merriam-Webster uses "good sense" to define wisdom. Wisdom is having knowledge, the good sense of knowing what to do and what not to do. Knowing when to move and when to be still. Wisdom will protect us when faith pushes us.

Wisdom is the ability to think and do what is reasonable and logical. Wisdom won't allow us to create a situation we can't handle. When we exercise wisdom we think, plan, consult, and wait. Faith fuels wisdom, and wisdom guides faith. The two need each other. Without faith, wisdom has no work to do; without our wisdom, the product of faith may not last.

God gave us faith and wisdom, and it's our job to use them interdependently, in conjunction with each other. We don't want to allow one to overpower the other, and we certainly don't want to use one and neglect the other. When we aren't using them both, God sometimes makes the call for us. In my life, He recognizes I have faith and exercise it quite often, but sometimes He steps in when it comes to wisdom. He may say, "She lacks patience, she's not ready for children." Because of His infinite wisdom, He makes me wait.

God knows us, He created us, and whether we feel like it or not, He's with us always. He knows what we're ready for and those things we're not. It doesn't matter how much we try to convince Him because He always operates with wisdom.

Faith will get us what we desire and using wisdom will secure it and ensure it's ours for the keeping. We all want what we want when we want it, but if we are to maintain what He has shown us, the things He releases to us, the gifts He bestows on us, we must apply faith and employ wisdom. It's when we use them both that we begin to see our little girl arise.

## Prayer

Father God,

In all things I know I should have faith, even when I can't see it, I should believe it to be. When I operate in faith, I'm encouraged that all You've promised will manifest. Even if not right away, I believe it will come to pass at some point. Lord, help me to remain in faith, even when it looks and feels like it's not going to happen. Even when it takes longer than expected, help me to maintain at the very least a mustard seed size of faith, and allow it to grow throughout the process. God, not only do I want faith, I need wisdom. I need wisdom to know what to do while I wait in faith, to make the best choices while I wait, and when the wait is over, help me to apply wisdom, so I won't mess up what faith helped produce. God, Your word says, the people perish because of a lack of knowledge; knowledge is wisdom.

I don't want to perish, so I ask that You grace me with wisdom, Your wisdom. Increase my understanding and awareness. Give me wisdom to make good choices, wisdom to know when to go and when to stay, wisdom to know when to speak and when to be silent, wisdom to know how to respond, and wisdom to follow Your guidance. Doing it my way has proven unsuccessful multiple times, but Lord, You're all knowing. When I adhere to what you advise, I know that I will be successful every time. I am asking that as I arise, I do so with faith and wisdom, and that the two operate in my life continuously.

### Workbook Reminder

Don't forget to complete the activities in your *Little Girl Arise* Workbook, which will help us recognize the need for both faith and wisdom. When we arise to operate in our purpose, we need them both. One without the other is an unequal equation. God wants us to be equipped with both. Faith plus Wisdom, that's a winning combination.

# Little Girl Arise

## Chapter 7:

### Distractions

Don't you hate it when you're making significant progress, you're waiting on God to answer your prayers, you're being faithful and working towards accomplishing your goals, and then suddenly it happens? It hits you out of nowhere, and you can't seem to ignore it. That annoying urge to do something completely different. Something that's not aligned with what you should be doing and won't bring you any gain. Be careful, it's the ugly monster known as distraction.

Distractions are often presented as obstacles set to take us off course. They disrupt our focus, interfere with our determination, and negatively impact our motivation. You may find that your distraction will automatically become a matter of importance, and what you should focus on will get pushed to the side, no longer being a priority.

Don't get me wrong, not all distractions are bad. There are times you'll have welcomed distractions. For example, let's say you've been working on an extremely tedious project and your husband or significant other stops by for an impromptu lunch date. Maybe your relationship has been in a bad place and putting him off will only add more strain to an already sensitive situation. In this case, the distraction is needed, but that's not the distraction we'll focus on in this chapter. The distraction for this chapter is the kind that causes you to stop progressing towards your goals, the types of distraction that interrupts your pursuit of fulfilling purpose.

This distraction comes along just as you've decided to renew your relationship with God. The relationship that requires you to spend time with Him, praying, meditating, and reading your devotional. Be very careful because distractions can be very sneaky. It doesn't always present itself as loud and annoying; sometimes it comes quiet and peacefully. When you begin to delve into your devotional, distraction comes to you in the form of sleepiness. This distraction tells you that it isn't a good time for reading, praying, or meditating because you're too tired. When you give in to that, the distraction has won. It's caused you to lose focus on what's important-- the nurturing of your relationship with God.

Don't feel embarrassed. I've allowed distractions to deter my focus many times. At some point or another, we all give in to distractions, forget about our initial focus, and eventually, it's no longer a priority on our list of things to do. The question is what are you willing to lose that's worth the distraction you've welcomed?

Many of you will probably answer with a firm, *"Nothing."* However, we do it more than we actually think. You may not recognize it as a distraction because we've become accustomed to renaming it to make us feel better. Instead of saying you're distracted, you may say you're taking a break (which is sometimes needed for rejuvenation purposes, but sometimes a means of procrastination). An interruption, a pause, whatever you name it, if you don't get back to your primary focus, you've sacrificed something you would have gained had you stayed focused. Therefore, you must learn to be attentive and mindful of distractions, so they don't interfere with *arising*. Here are a few recommendations for handling distractions while trying to arise.

First, you must be able to identify a distraction. If you're focused on one thing, and something completely different comes along and demands your focus (there's a difference between demands and requirements), then it's likely a distraction. Remember, a distraction is something that'll take your attention away from that which requires your attention and energy, at that time.

Once you identify what distractions are, and since you know they'll come, it's wise to plan how you'll respond. Perhaps you're working on a very important project for work, and one of your good friends calls for help. She's preparing to attend an event and *needs* you to go shopping with her. What do you do? You love to shop, and she needs your feedback. You begin to convince yourself that this could be a major fail if you don't go help her out because her sense of style isn't always on point.

When you plan for the distraction, you're assessing if the distraction will benefit you in any way. *Should I really stop what I'm working on to take a shopping trip? Can I do it later or is it necessary to be done right away?* If it can wait, it's likely a distraction;

therefore, maintain focus and ignore that distraction. It's okay to compromise. Try saying something like, *"Girl, I have to get this proposal done, but I can go with you this evening or tomorrow."* Or even, *"Remember that big project at work I told you about? Yes girl, I'm working on that right now. If you can't go later, send me pictures of your options, and I'll let you know what I think."* You can still help your friend, but at the same time resist giving in to the distraction of a mini-shopping trip in the middle of being productive.

Controlling distractions begins with self-control. Don't allow distractions to dictate your actions and progress. You must know when to say no, when to ignore the call, when to make necessary changes, and how to do so quickly. Too much time toying with distractions is a distraction. When the phone rings, sitting and wondering, "hmm should I answer that? I wonder what she wants?" is a distraction. Don't spend time asking those questions in your mind. It will only slow you down.

Identify distractions, plan for distractions, prepare your response to distractions, use self-control to manage distractions, and finally, pace yourself to avoid distractions. Don't overwhelm yourself. Don't sit at the desk and attempt to write the book in one sitting. When it's your first time planning an event, don't sit and try to plan the entire event in an hour. Don't try to find the answers to all of life's problems in one day; it takes time to resolve that type of complexity. You must give yourself a reasonable amount of time to accomplish any task. Even God paced Himself when creating the earth, so why do we think we can do it all at one time?

You must allow yourself a break at times. Remember breaks are always necessary for rejuvenation purposes. Work becomes overwhelming, family is demanding, relationships require a considerable amount of your attention, but bare in mind, there's a very important need to implement self-care. Distractions easily creep in when you feel overworked. They creep in and stay for extended periods of time because you're so inundated that you may become frustrated and no longer want to focus on the task. *We're over it.* When this happens it's easy to give in to the distraction with no immediate plans to regain focus.

When you've applied the maximum pressure that you can stand, it's wise to take a breather. Productivity and efficiency significantly decrease when you don't allow yourself time to relax. I like to call it a brain break. A planned break is not a distraction. It's an integral part of your plan that will help keep your attention on the matter at hand. The break is necessary for consistency and efficiency.

So, by now you may be asking, "what does any of this have to do with *Little Girl Arise*? How can this help that spot in me that is dead, the part lying dormant; the part of me that needs to arise?" Well, the purpose of distractions is to prevent progress in all areas of your life, not just work and relationships. When you're trying to live again, distractions of past hurt and pain resurface; you may recognize them as memories of all the things that didn't go well for you, all those things that hurt and disappointed you, and all those times it didn't work out in your favor. When you are trying to extend or receive forgiveness, the distraction of all the ways you were wronged prevents you from living a life of forgiveness. When you're trying to move forward and make essential progress, the distraction of previous failure *conveniently* steps in to keep you right where you are.

Distractions are meant to prevent you from giving your full attention to any one thing; especially if it's something relative to fulfilling your purpose. If you're focused on your past, you won't be able to arise. Identifying the distraction, planning your response, using self-control, and pacing yourself are all concepts used to manage physical distractions, but you must also apply them in managing internal and mental distractions as well. Sometimes these are the most dangerous forms of distractions.

They're the distractions that tell you what you can't do. The distractions of uncomfortable memories, which replay in our minds causing us to feel discouraged then deciding not to try because we haven't been successful with previous attempts. The distractions that show us all the reasons why we might as well stay in the place that we are in and dissuades us from living again.

If you are going to arise, you must prepare for every tactic, every obstacle, and every barrier that will try to keep you where you are. You must be prepared to say no to a loved one, ignore a naysayer, lose a friend, temporarily stand alone, and maybe even be knocked down multiple times having to get right back up. It's not preparing for the worst but preparing for the work; the work required for you to arise.

Informing you that distractions will occur during this process gives you the upper hand. You can begin developing your plan now. You can begin working on your response. You can begin practicing your *"no."* Better yet, you can begin practicing how to ignore.

When you are truly ready to arise, you will make up your mind that nothing will stop you. You won't be deterred, you won't be discouraged, you won't be dismayed, and you won't be distracted. You're going to limit the distractions, give your full attention to your goal, make arising your priority, and in no time, Little Girl, you'll do just that, Arise.

## *Prayer*

Father God, I know the enemy will send distractions along my journey to discourage me and to keep me from making progress in the pursuit of my purpose. I ask that You help me recognize distractions, ignore the distractions, and remain on task. I ask that You help me focus on the things You have called me to do. Strengthen my ability to ignore disruptions and resist interruptions. When I try on my own, I'm not always successful, but I know if You help me, if You keep my mind where it needs to be, if You help me resist then I can defeat distractions and stay focused on what's in front of me. I don't want to prolong my journey, so it's important that I don't get sidetracked. Whether it's friends or family, work or social engagements, or even tiredness or frustration, I will not succumb to distractions. I will remain focused. Lord, if I get tired, if I get weary, I will allow myself a break, but I assure You I'll get back to it. I want to fulfill my purpose, and to do so, I must eliminate distractions. In Jesus Name. Amen.

## Workbook Reminder

Don't forget to complete the activities in your *Little Girl Arise* Workbook, which will assist in strategizing to avoid distractions. You'll be amazed at how much planning your response to distractions, ahead of time, will improve your ability to remain focused when distractions arise.

# Little Girl Arise

## Chapter 8:
### Silence

As I stated in the previous chapter, sometimes distractions can come in many forms, and in some cases, it comes in the form of unnecessary chaos--situations that get out of hand or go in the wrong direction simply because no one was willing to be silent and listen. Being silent isn't easy, but there's power in silence. It takes more self-control and discipline to remain silent when you want to tell someone off.

I may not always *listen* when advice is given, but I'm a pretty good listener. Instead of saying I didn't listen to my mom's advice about attending my baby shower, I should've said I didn't use wisdom and listen *to understand*. Along with not listening, I have the tendency to talk too much. There are days that I talk so much I get on my own nerves. It's hard to listen and talk at the same time, but I'm sure you're already aware of that fact.

In graduate school during my practicum experience, I asked my professor to observe one of my sessions. I needed his input because a couple of my peers had given me some very harsh feedback in between sessions, and honestly, I wanted to quit. If I was as horrible as they made me feel, I needed to hurry and change program tracts, so I'd still be able to graduate at the expected time. My next move depended on my professor's feedback. If he agreed with them, then that would've been the confirmation I needed that counseling wasn't the field for me.

The client finally arrived, and I began my session. As soon as those fifty minutes were over, I quickly made my way to his office for feedback. I sat in the chair across from him and braced myself. He didn't hold back. He gave me his honest feedback about my session.

"Tarkisha, you talk too much. You worked harder than your client for most of the session. You don't need to change tracts; you need to stop talking so much. You must be okay with silence. When it's silent, the client may be processing. However, if you keep talking, then the client won't have the chance to process." I took that constructive feedback, and after that, I talked a lot less in sessions.

Eleven years ago, that didn't mean what it means to me as I reflect on his words, *you have to be okay with silence. When it's silent, the client may be processing. However, if you keep talking, then the client won't have the chance to process.* He was right; I wasn't okay with silence. When the client didn't respond, I thought it was my turn. Even today, it takes thirty minutes to start my sessions or session goes over time because the client and I talk.

Talking is great. We need to talk. For some things, we must open our mouths and speak, but when we're speaking, we must be very mindful of what we say. Before you allow it to leave your voice box and part your lips, think about it first. When I was a child, too much talking in class resulted in me getting a whipping once my mom received my conduct sheet. Talking as a counselor prolongs my client's session, and personally, there have been times talking has cost me opportunities and relationships. Not necessarily because I was talking too much, but because of what came out when I spoke. God is still working on me there.

The Bible tells us in Ecclesiastes 3:7, *"A time to keep silence, and a time to speak up."* The Message translation says, *"A right time to shut up and another to speak up."* It's of the utmost importance that you're capable of knowing the time to speak and the time to be silent. You may want to justify and clarify, you want to be understood, you want others to hear you out, and you want to get your point across; trust me, I know, I feel the same way. However, over the years I've learned a very valuable lesson, and it may sound strange, but trust me when I tell you most times silence gets more attention than noise.

There will be times that your silence will make the point you so badly want to open your mouth to make. At times silence allows the opportunity to give thought without distractions, resulting in better decisions and choices and fewer consequences. There will be times when silence will get you out of the trouble speaking got you into. Sometimes silence is the key that opens our next door, but we remain locked out because it's the key we always seem to lose.

Many times, I've been in a place of frustration where I wanted to step out of character; I wanted to say and do things that I knew I shouldn't. During these times, I should be exercising faith, patience, and maintaining my confidence in God. I'd get so irritated because waiting is already hard, and when you find yourself dealing with things and facing trials and tribulations while waiting, it has a way of triggering agitation. I'd be easily irritated and everything people did made me mad. I'd feel like I want to say something, I need to say something, and I have to say something, so I would decide to say something.

In the past, when I opened my mouth, I intentionally struck to hurt. I gathered words and phrases that made others feel like they were hit. In fact, the person on the receiving end of my words probably would've preferred a physical fight. My words were so harsh, I knew an apology was pointless because if it were me, I wouldn't allow anyone to talk to me that way, and I certainly wouldn't be ready to accept an apology right away.

One night, I found myself in a situation that made me want to say everything I was holding inside. In my mind, I had been silent long enough. Before I could open my mouth to speak, the Holy Spirit quickly convicted me and reminded me about this book, which I was still writing at the time. Immediately, I had to stop and pray, "God, help me live and be an example of what I'm teaching."

It doesn't matter who you are or the titles you hold, flesh is flesh, and every now and then it rises, even in the best of us. That night, I was close to the edge, but the Holy Spirit stopped me. Afterward, I remember texting my friend, an accountability partner, telling her that I was so angry. I said, *"but you know what, I'm not going to respond. I'm not going to allow the devil to interfere with my purpose."* I had to quickly recognize the enemy and his tactics. He was waiting on me to open my mouth and make noise that would cause division.

That night I was reminded when we're doing what we're supposed to do, when we're in God's will; when we're walking it, talking it, and truly living it, the devil is going to throw anything he can at us to cause interference. He thinks he's so smart and knows what to do. He knows exactly who to send. He knows exactly what to make them do. He knows exactly what buttons to press. He tries to use those tactics, which usually trigger us to speak out instead of praying, so he can throw us off, deter us, mess with our faith, disturb our peace, ultimately interrupting and causing interference between us and purpose.

Recognize when it's the enemy! Little girls, recognize when he's trying to destroy, stop, break, and interfere with anything God ordained in your life. It could be a job, a goal you've set, a ministry, a relationship, or a business. He's not picky, neither is he considerate; whatever he can use to knock you down so that you are less motivated to arise, that's where he's aiming. When you learn to identify his tactics and techniques, then you can better respond. The night I referred to earlier in this chapter, I used silence.

When you're silent, the enemy is thrown off. He doesn't know what you're doing, he doesn't know what you're thinking, he doesn't know your next move, but that's only if you're silent. If you're responding all the time, he's taking that and planning against what you've spoken. He's sneaky and nosey so don't even try to whisper. In the nicest way I can say it, just shut up. When I recognized my ability to keep my mouth closed, even when silence wasn't my first choice, I was confident, my little girl was arising.

## Prayer

Father,

Our most common reaction in almost every situation in life is to open our mouths and respond. We engage in arguments, say things that are hurtful, threaten others, and let our mouths get us in all sorts of trouble we had no actual plans for. Just as we are quick to anger, we are, in many cases, much quicker to speak. I'm learning that I don't have to respond to everything that's said or done to me. I don't have to say a word. I'm learning I can allow my silence to do the work for me. When I keep my mouth closed, I'm able to think clearer and make better decisions before making a response. When I keep my mouth closed, I'm able to allow myself and others time to process. When I keep my mouth closed, I'm more likely to keep a situation positive than allowing negativity to creep in when I speak. But I need Your help, Lord. I need You to help me distinguish between the times I should speak and the times I should remain quiet, because it's so much easier for me to speak than to not say a word. However, if silence will help my little girl arise, I need to use it more often, and with Your help and guidance, I will. In Jesus Name. Amen.

## *Workbook Reminder*

I want us to all gain a better understanding of the benefit of silence. It's a powerful tool we neglect way too often. Don't forget to complete the activities in your *Little Girl Arise* Workbook concerning silence. Together, we will learn why Ecclesiastes 3:7 advises that there is a time to keep silent. For some of us, it's not easy, but at times, it's a necessity.

# Chapter 9:
## Watch What You Say

It would be unrealistic if we were expected to remain silent the entire time we went through a period of trials. It would be ideal, but realistically, it's nearly impossible. Naturally, we want to talk about what we're going through. We want to vent, complain, rationalize, scream, and shout. Simply put, we want to be heard, and we often sense a pressing need to get it out to anyone that will listen.

Talking about what's bothering us or causing us to feel overwhelmed is healthy; to be totally honest, it's necessary. When we internalize our mind begins to take us places we never would've gone had we just called our mother, sister, friend or mentor and said "look, I need to talk. I have a lot going on, and I just need to get it out." Holding our feelings in or trying to suppress them is what normally leads to anger, depression, anxiety, suicide, homicide, isolation, etc. We figure no one wants to hear what we have to say, and if they did listen, we question if they truly care.

As a counselor, of course I think talking is a significant part of the healing process; if you don't get your story out, there's no way to address it. I believe when you let things out you're able to better process, think, and make healthier decisions. You can hear the perspective of others, you can get feedback on how you should proceed, or even just have someone demonstrate how much they care about you by taking the time to simply listen.

So yes, talking out our worries, frustrations, and concerns is good, and a necessary component of the healing and arising. However, it's extremely important that we are mindful of what we say. Do you all mind if I briefly discuss watching what you say when you do speak? Many times, while going through situations that are unwelcomed, uncomfortable, and more than likely unfortunate, we become reckless with our words. Our tongue is powerful, and the words we use can promote life or cause death, our words can shed light or bring about darkness, our words can better a situation or cause it to be blown out of proportion and bigger than what it was ever meant to be. Therefore, we must be mindful of what we say when experiencing those difficult moments in life that we often feel were designed to break us. Consider this, your place of burden has the potential to transform into your ministry of breakthrough, but you must be mindful of the words you speak while you're in a place or situation you'd rather not be.

I've always been told not to complain about where I am in life or what I might be going through, but that's always been a challenge for me. *Are you kidding? Don't complaint and I have all this crap going on? I mean come on; it's one thing after the other.* Sometimes complaining seems like the only thing that gives me relief, but the word complaining does sound bad, right? Therefore, I changed my vocabulary and the intentions behind what was once identified as complaining; I now refer to it as releasing or venting. However, if you know me, and know me well, you know that at the end of a venting session, at the end of the release, at the end of complaining, there's also problem solving. I do it with my clients, therapists I supervise, family and friends, and yes, even with myself.

I wholeheartedly believe in getting it out, expressing yourself, and making sure you don't leave anything in to fester and cause mental or emotional damage. However, after the vent is done I always transition to problem solving. I rarely allow anyone to leave session without problem solving and devising a plan, at least having somewhere to start. I call this *productive venting*. They leave a little bit lighter because they were able to release their load, but they're also equipped with a plan to address the situation. They get all of their *bad talk* out and are ready to progress to action. Complaining doesn't resolve any issues or get you out of the trial quicker; learning the lesson and doing something about it allows us to experience progress.

Here are a few tips to consider when you're *productively venting*. This'll help you vent with a purpose. After venting, you're then able to move along into acceptance and problem solving. Eventually, you'll realize that you've pressed through the situation that once held you captive, had you defeated, and depleted you. Your words can keep you in an uncomfortable position much longer than you need to be. If you think about these tips while venting, you'll be able to release and begin working your way out of the storm without complaining. *Productive venting*; however, no complaining.

1.    <u>Remember in some way all test are timed, and the time will eventually expire;</u> you won't have to endure it forever. You'll survive that storm, you'll recover from that loss, you'll have a second chance; however, what you say may keep you there longer than necessary. When you speak, speak life not death; speak victory, not defeat; and do so from the voice of a survivor not a victim. Yes, even before you've survived it, begin to speak from the position of a survivor.

2.    <u>Before you speak, *think*.</u> We rarely do this; here's how it goes for some of us: something happens, without any thought we open our mouths and words and phrases come out, we later gather the facts only to find out we reacted too soon. Of course, we feel bad for what we said, but it's too late because that noisy hole in our face, we refer to it as the mouth, has already done the dirty work. I teach my clients to STOP, THINK then RESPOND. Stopping to think gives you the opportunity to process your words, and really consider if responding is actually necessary. While you're thinking you're able to ask yourself if your words will help or hurt the situation, will they serve a purpose, will they produce anything good? If a response is deemed necessary, then at least you've given yourself time to calm down and process the response; it could prevent things from escalating to a place of no return.

3.    You've heard *it's not what you say, but how you say it*? <u>We must be cautious of how we speak to or about our situation, those connected to us during that situation, and most importantly to self.</u> The Bible tells us in Ephesians 4:15 to speak the truth in love. Our delivery is everything. Screaming and shouting, using profanity and sarcasm, being condescending, negative, and passive aggressive might feel good while we're using them. We may even think we're getting our point across; but in most situations, when we use these tactics, the person on the other end of our words have already tuned us out before we ever really get to the real point. I've made my loved ones aware *it's okay to correct me, but please do so in love*; otherwise, I have difficulty receiving it. If you want people to hear you, you must speak to them like their attention is appreciated, not demanded.

4.        In some cases, a response is unnecessary. It's not going to make a difference; it could potentially make matters worse. In those situations, grab a pen and a few sheets of paper, and let it out there. Writing is so much better than speaking. Speaking can get you in trouble; however, when you write it, no one ever has to see it, you don't have to share it with a soul, but you are able to get it out. Write it then tear it up or burn it. If you know that your venting won't be productive, but hazardous, then reserve your words for paper; don't launch them…you don't want them to ricochet back to you.

5.        Don't do all the talking, use your ears and <u>listen</u>. For most of us, the problem is that we talk too much and listen too little. We have this back and forth pointless exchange of words, in which no one has been heard; therefore, there was no point in speaking in the first place. You learn and resolve conflict or disagreements quicker when you listen.

Too many times I've allowed my words to put me in positions that I never wanted to be. I've said things that people haven't forgotten. I've said things that people chose to forgive, but then distanced themselves; truthfully, I don't blame them. Speaking ill of your situation and recklessly to others doesn't benefit you at all; it prolongs your fulfillment of purpose. When you speak, build yourself up, use positive and uplifting words. Little Girl, if you want to arise, if you want to live again, you must speak life to you, your situation, and those connected to you.

## *Prayer*

Father, when I'm going through a difficult season of life or faced with a challenging situation, I tend to say things I really don't mean. I speak from a place of pain, frustration, and anger, instead of declaring positivity and victory over that which I'm experiencing. Please help guide the words I speak to others and over myself at all times, especially when I'm in the midst of what seem unbearable. Help me to recognize if it's necessary to respond, and if so, help me bridle my tongue, choose my words wisely, and shape my delivery. It's not my goal to hurt or attack others; therefore, I have to be mindful of the words I speak. When I open my mouth to say something that isn't positive or productive, cut me off, don't allow me to open my mouth, remind me of the consequences I'll face, and how my little girl may never arise if I'm reckless with my words. In Jesus Name. Amen.

## Workbook Reminder

Words are powerful, and how we use them can be even more damaging. It's crucial that we be mindful of what we say and how we say it. Let's take some time to choose our words wisely and evaluate our tone and delivery. In your *Little Girl Arise* workbook, there are a few activities that will help you increase your awareness about the *words you speak and exactly how you should speak them*. Don't miss the opportunity to begin reframing what you say and how you say it.

# Little Girl Arise

## Chapter 10:
### You're Not Alone

November 2, 2005, the day my son died, I felt like I was the only mother in the world that had suffered the loss of a child. I didn't consider the possibility that there were any other grieving mothers in the world. All the mothers I knew personally had their child/children. I felt alone and isolated. I felt like no one could ever understand the pain I was experiencing. I just knew I'd have to go through this season of loss alone; I honestly thought I had no one to talk to that could relate. I knew there would be things in life that I'd have to face all by myself, but losing my first-born child, which I carried to term, was not something I ever thought I'd experience, and certainly not alone.

If I didn't have faith, hadn't been raised with a solid biblical foundation, and didn't have a personal relationship with my Father, I probably would've lost my mind. I didn't need it anyway... or so I thought. I mean, who needs a mind when your world just crashed and burned, when everything you ever wanted was taken from you when your *new* reason for living just died. I sure didn't. I didn't need a mind, a heart, a body; I didn't need anything except the one thing that was not coming back, my Jayden. But because I had a relationship with Jesus, and I am one of His favorite daughters, He positioned people in my life that day, and each day since, to remind me that I'm not alone.

Most of the people that encouraged me hadn't experienced the same loss as I did; however, they experienced some form of loss that had a detrimental effect on them, just as my loss had on me. Some hadn't experienced a loss at all; they just loved me and seeing me hurt, hurt them. Some wanted to fight. Some cried with me. Most sat in silence because they weren't so sure what to say or what to do. Seeing me cry was nothing new for them, but seeing me silent, that's something they weren't used to. Something they weren't sure how to handle.

My parents, sisters, grandparents, and many family members sacrificed time and sleep. So many people reached out. So many people were there for me during my time of need. My sorors and frat brothers, people I hadn't talked to in quite some time, even people I didn't know, but they knew of me. They were all there for me at one time or another, in some form or another. No one missed an opportunity to remind me that I was loved, if I needed anything I could count on each of them, and that I was not alone.

Remembering all that takes me back; I allow myself that every now and then. However, it also reminds me that in traumatic situations, when we think others are so far removed, we're not alone. I've learned that a person doesn't have to go through the exact situation that I've gone through to understand, to be empathic, or to be a support. It's nice when we have a survivor of the same crisis in our corner, but that may not always be the case.

Support is an integral component of survival. You may think that you're able to get through every challenge life throws at you without having to ask anyone for help, but that's highly unlikely. There will be times you'll need a person to listen as you spill out your frustrations. You'll need someone to sit on the phone with you in silence. You may need someone that's willing to get up in the middle of the night to offer comfort. I needed them all. At times, I didn't want to make the call; I wanted to do it on my own. But it never failed, God would always send someone, whether they knew it or not, and just their presence would take a little piece of that load off of me.

It was the small things that meant so much during those days, and even now. I remember Jayden's birthday in 2017. It was on a Sunday, and I was broken. I had to go through that day, my baby's birthday, without him again. I didn't want to go to church, but had I stayed home it would've been to engage in a pity party. I cried throughout the entire service. I remember the Holy Spirit showing up that Sunday. A comforting spirit lingered throughout the sanctuary even after the service was over; people weren't leaving, we just spent time sitting in the presence of the One we needed the most at that very moment.

While sitting there with my eyes closed, I felt someone sit down next to me, place their arm around me, and hug me. He never said a word, he just sat a minute, placed his arm around my shoulder, pulled me in a little as a daddy would do his daughter, and hugged me; something I never got from Jayden on his birthday or any other day. I'm pretty sure he had no clue that a good hug was my antidote, but God knew. When I'm going through something, a hug tends to make a world of difference. Isn't it just like God to send exactly what we need, when we need it, even when we don't realize or admit that we need it? That Sunday He sent my Pastor.

During difficult moments in life, God doesn't want us to isolate from others. He doesn't want us to withdraw. God wants us to lean on one another, support one another, and encourage one another; just when we think we don't have anyone that can provide those things, He'll send someone. That person serves as a reminder, little girl, you're not alone.

I don't know what caused your dying moment. I don't know the exact thing that has your little girl trapped inside of you, dreading the thought of living again. Your moment may not have been like mine. Or maybe it was. Your moment could've come from the divorce of your parents; your own failed marriage; death of a loved one; betrayal by someone you were loyal to; symptoms and responses to mental illness; sexual molestation or abuse; domestic violence, or many more tragedies. Maybe you tried to die. Attempted taking your own life, and when it wasn't successful, you remained stuck there, in what you might call misery. Misery that would one day create a completely different meaning than you'd ever expect.

I don't know when your moment occurred or what happened to cause it; I don't know why it happened to you, and I don't know what you felt while experiencing it. I empathize with you, and as a survivor of *death while living,* I want you to know how deeply sorry I am that you had to experience that in life. I want you to know that though you thought it was meant to destroy you, you will soon find out it was designed to propel you into purpose. Not only you, but also set things in motion for others to follow.

In case you've forgotten, allow me to remind you that you're human. Know this, it's okay to cry, it's okay to have a moment, and yes, it's okay to be angry; just don't live there. Experience and express those feelings, own those feelings, address those feelings, and control those feelings. Don't allow them to control you. There were many days I sat alone in a dark room crying because I didn't want to bother anyone. That was a trick of the enemy to keep me isolated. God always outsmarted him and sent someone to interrupt the isolation. I didn't *need* to be alone, I didn't *have* to be alone, and despite what I tried to swindle myself into believing, I really didn't *want* to be alone. You know what, even when I thought I was, I was never truly alone.

I may not know the cause of your *death*; however, I do know with a source of support, your lifeless situation can be placed on *life support* until you recover, regain your strength, and find the will to live and desire to arise. Gather your supports. Gather them now before you encounter the next situation that tries to take you out. You'll have them in place, ready to provide First Aid and CPR if the situation loses consciousness and has no sign of breathing.

Please don't attempt to survive a situation that's sucking the life from you, by yourself. You cannot. You may not survive. Have you ever seen someone who's not breathing perform CPR on themselves? Or someone that performed their own surgical operation? When you're fighting for your life, it's necessary that you have someone that can help nurse you back to life. In a medical emergency, patients have doctors or nurses; in my life crisis I had family and friends, and later in life, my therapist. Had I tried reviving myself, by myself, I probably wouldn't have survived.

Here's the good news as it relates to supports: you get to design and structure your support system, but the key is to build wisely. Be mindful of whom you engage and connect with because one of them may have to step up in an emergency, and you need strong friends; you don't want them to flake during this time. I have about ten people that I know without a doubt; if I go down, they're well prepared to provide rescue breathing (prayer) and chest compressions (encouragement) to revive me. They don't need full details of the situation, they aren't asking questions, they're going right to what they know I need, and what they know will position me to regain breathing and consciousness. They're determined to see me live and fulfill my purpose; they're not letting me die before my time.

I have spiritual fighters; and some not so spiritual fighters…it's okay, laugh a little. I have a team that sets me up for life. There's someone that will immediately stop and pray. There's another that will say they're coming over and there's no stopping them. There's one that will say, "Come on, let's go, you need to get out." And there are a few that'll ask, "Who did it and where are they?" There are a couple that'll sit on the phone and allow me to control the conversation. And all of them, each one of them, acknowledge the strength they see in me and reminds me of it, especially when I can't see it in myself.

While I'm there, lifeless on the floor, stuck between leaving and staying, living and dying, they're whispering, "Come on Kisha, do you remember when God brought you through this? Alright Kisha, come back, do you know the strength you have, do I need to remind you? Kisha, such and such is depending on you, you have to pull through." They recall the many things I survived, the things I've overcome, and reminded me, "Remember when this happened, and it didn't take you out. Depression won't take you out. Anger won't take you out. Frustration won't take you out. And this won't either!"

I'd be leaving out a special addition to my support team if I failed to mention the few that don't talk; they've never said a word. These three love me with a love so unconditional, so authentic, so genuine; a love that every person should have the opportunity to experience. I call them Sugar Ray, Spencer Reid, and Cassius Flash, my three beautiful boxer babies. I truly believe God brought them to me, so my alone and lonely days could come to an end. He knows all about me, He brought them when He knew my natural, physical supporters would begin to slim down. Having those three around made the change in relationships a little less noticeable and a lot less painful, and while at it, smothered me with so much love.

Having a support system isn't optional; it's a necessity. Whether we want to accept it or not, at some point we will need people. Be mindful of who you choose. It's imperative that you build wisely; these are people, which at some point, you may have to depend on. I can't have weak people; I need strong friends. I can't have wishy-washy people; I need those who are confident and sure. I can't have lazy people; I need those that are motivated and have some ambition about themselves. I can't have negative people; there's just no need for them. I have my team, I can call them by name, and when a fatal situation occurs, I know who to go to. My support system is solid, and it's a must that it remains that way. With them, every time a situation knocks me down, I do not doubt this little girl will arise.

Prayer

Lord God, You did not create me to be alone or to face every situation in life by myself. You did not create me to isolate and try to figure out every detail with no input or guidance from others. Father, You love me so much that You've placed people on earth to stand in the gap when I can't stand for myself. You've placed people in my life that recognize who I am, and when they notice I'm not carrying myself accordingly, they call me out on it and hold me accountable. I pray that You designate people that will listen to me vent, but at the end of it help me find the solution to my problem. I thank You for those that You have afforded me, those that You've assigned to me. I ask that You help me identify those people so that as I'm building my support system, I'm building it with believers, people that are loyal, people that are consistent, people that are dependable, and people that are genuine. I'm asking that You help me identify the right people and not counterfeits. I ask that You help me identify people that will pray with and for me without asking questions. Lord, I know that I always have You, You're always with me wherever I am and through whatever is going on in my life. But thank You for using people to help me through as well; people that remind me I am not alone in the fight of my life. Father, just as people serve as supports for me, I ask that I grow to stand in the gap for others. I thank You that I too will be a support to others, reminding them that they aren't alone either. In Jesus Name. Amen.

## *Little Girl Arise*

### *Workbook Reminder*

In your *Little Girl Arise workbook*, there are a few activities to help shape and guide you to developing a solid support system, one that will without a doubt show up and stand in the gap when they're needed.

# Chapter 11:
## Tell Your Story

Remember in Ecclesiastes 3 we learned there's a right time to shut up and another to speak up? Allow me to introduce you to one of those times to speak.

I'm sorry to burst your bubble, someone once burst mine as well, but I feel the need to tell you what someone once told me: "Your situation wasn't just for you. Someone else needs to hear it." It took a while for me to process that information and make it make sense to me. I understood the words, but I didn't understand why I had to suffer for someone else to survive. Wow! Kind of like Jesus did for us on the cross. Now understand, I'm in no way comparing us to Jesus, but the point is if He had to suffer, then why wouldn't we? What makes us so special?

Our Father is quite meticulous in the way He does things. If I didn't have experiences that caused pain, eventually pushing me to pray, to forgive, to use faith and wisdom, to call on and use supports, to lay aside every distraction, to learn when to be silent and always be mindful of what I say, and to pursue purpose then I couldn't model for my sisters, friends, family members, clients, mentees, or anyone else how to push through and survive their life crises.

I'm not the only one God has or will use to help the next person. He's also using you. Yes, you! That dreadful circumstance that almost took you out, it's not just for you. It's for your bestie, your niece, and your lunch buddy at work. It's for your prayer partner, your daughter, and your neighbor. It's for the friends you always go out with, the ones that seem to have it all together, but in reality, they don't. It's for people you least expect, and some you don't even know yet. Your story of pain, prevailing, and purpose is not only for you; it's also for other women.

Your mistakes could stop someone else from doing the same not so smart thing, making the same unwise choices, and acting the same foolish way you once did. Our life lessons may serve as a guide for some little girl that's headed down the same crooked path we journeyed, but still has time to get back on track before she's too far gone. In order to learn from her mother, her grandmother, her friend, from me; for her to learn from you, we have to open our mouths.

You can't be ashamed of what happened to you; you can't protect and hide your scars, you can't go through things, survive them and say, "Whew, glad that's over, let me move on with life." You can't be selfish with your experiences. For the sake of the little girl watching you, you must open your mouth and share your story; and not just for her, but for you as well. When you and I remain silent, especially about those deep dark things that you never want to shed light on, you remain in bondage to that thing. Opening our mouths will break cycles, break generational curses, and help so many little girls break free and arise.

Those of us, who are now Arisen Little Girls, must tell our story, and we have to do so in a meaningful, purposeful way. Not a pitiful, "come on feel sorry for me" kind of way. Not in a bitter or resentful way. You must model your story in a way that shows others that survival is possible, recovery is possible, getting back in the game is possible, and arising is possible. If you're not going to share your story in these uplifting, motivating, encouraging ways, then that's a time you should exercise silence until you're ready.

Sharing your story will motivate another little girl to arise. When she hears strength, courage, joy, peace, love, and victory in your voice she opens her eyes. As you continue to declare what you've conquered, with the help of the Lord, her limbs, which may have been paralyzed and lifeless, will begin to tingle and regain movement. When she hears you say, "I choose life instead of death," her heart, which could've lost its rhythm, may suddenly begin to beat, and she'll feel the warm blood of Jesus running through her veins. At that point, she's arising because she saw you were able to get up and push forward after being knocked down. She's arising because you didn't hide behind fear, hurt, shame, or pain. She's arising because you demonstrated in action what she thought could never happen for her. She's arising because you simply opened your mouth and shared your story. She's arising, and that beautiful cycle will continue. Another little girl will arise because of her.

Little girls, we are not spiritually dead anymore; we are alive and well. We are fulfilling purpose, walking into our destiny, and living intentionally, unapologetically. I advise you to remove your cloak of death, trade it for a garment of praise, and victoriously, confidently and most of all, purposefully shout, "I'm no longer dead. I'm no longer asleep. What's in me is being resurrected. The little girl in me is not so little anymore. She's maturing. She knows who's she is; therefore, she knows who she is. My little girl, the one you used to see, she's no longer the same; she's arising. It's time because there's so much more for her to do."

Be bold and selfless enough to open your mouth, share your story, free yourself, and help another little girl that's living what you've gone through, endured, and survived, arise.

*Prayer*

Lord,

You know everything I've been through, and You know how it's affected me. Lord, I'm not always sure of why I've experienced all that I have, but if it is to help another little girl arise, help me share my story with boldness. Remove my concern that others may judge me or make fun of me. Remove my concern that I may be embarrassed or laughed at. Remove my concern of others being disappointed in me. If my life's journey will benefit someone else, help me tell my story with a purpose. Help me encourage someone else that they too can be a survivor and walk in victory after a life-threatening situation. You didn't allow me to go through what I went through and keep it only for myself. You want me to help others through my testimony of victory. I want others to survive just as I did, and when it is time, when it matters, and when it serves a great purpose, I will share exactly what happened and how I was able to continue to live in spite of the dying situations I experienced. In Jesus Name. Amen.

# Little Girl Arise

## Workbook Reminder

In your *Little Girl Arise* workbook, I want to help you begin to tell your story by helping you gain a better understanding of why you should tell your story. Don't forget to complete your activities on telling your story; it will change your life while saving another.

# Chapter 12:
## Tell Your Story - Little Girl Arise Spotlights

*I'm more than sure sharing your story will do so much for Little Girls everywhere.*

So often the parts of life that are uncomfortable restrain us; however, when God imparts purpose in you, He will not allow you to remain stagnant for too long. He shakes things up and makes it clear that what we may identify as misery, He's ordained for ministry. It's my prayer that *Little Girl Arise* promotes healing, the will to live, and the strength and desire to arise.

I pray that as you've read *Little Girl Arise,* and now begin to read the testimonies of the *Little Girl Arise Spotlights*, that you can begin your journey to arising. It's my prayer that each Little Girl who feels powerless finds strength because she now knows her sister, another Little Girl, was able to arise from that same situation. There's so much I'm asking God to do through *Little Girl Arise*, but most of all, I expect Him to do what He needs to do so that His little girls arise to fulfill their purpose!

As I was preparing to write my journey of pain, healing, purpose, and arising, the Holy Spirit impressed upon me to have four *Little Girls* share their stories of death while living. I didn't understand why He instructed me to ask others, and to be honest, I didn't know whom to ask; and if I did know, I figured they'd say no.

A few people came to mind; however, I prayed before proceeding because it was imperative that I incorporate who God had in mind. God is very careful of who He allows to pour into His daughters. He knows how valuable you, His little girls, are; therefore, He identified those that would speak life in spite of their encounter with death.

Reading the Little Girl Spotlight Moments reassured my certainty that I heard from God and aligned with His plan. I'm confident that He will use their *Little Girl Arise* moments to demonstrate that that which was meant to deter and destroy them, positioned them for purpose. And the same will happen for you. Little Girls of all ages, who thought life was over after their dying situation, will be encouraged, empowered, and equipped to live again, to arise.

To the ladies who accepted the charge, thank you for being transparent in sharing your journey with other little girls. I have expressed this to you many times, but I'd be remiss if I didn't thank each of you again. Your commitment continues to mean so much to me, and I'm more than sure your moment of arising will do so much for little girls everywhere. I continue to ask God for a special blessing and covering over your lives and all that you set out to do.

Your situations are personal to you, and didn't have to be shared; however, your willingness to say, "I'll use this to help another little girl", was such a selfless act! I am so glad to be connected to such strong arisen little girls like each of you. As I've always said, if you need me, you know how to reach me! I love each of you. God, I ask that You honor their sacrifice and bless their obedience, because of them many of your daughters will soon arise. I'm elated to introduce four Little Girls that were determined to Arise.

## Hope in Her

I truly believe as I recall my life and experiences that there's not been a moment that caused me to die. On the contrary, the collection of experiences that tried to take my life has so far proven to be unsuccessful. Even in my darkest moments, I knew somehow that I would make it out. That's the funny thing about faith.

When your world is falling apart, sometimes you can lose sight of faith because it gets lost amongst the rubble that's scattered at your feet. As Merriam-Webster would put it, faith is "a firm belief in something for which there is no proof." You see, despite periods of my life that looked like death, I always maintained a strong sense of faith. Not particularly faith in those around me, and not even faith in God sometimes, but faith in myself, that I was strong enough to make it out.

After enduring sexual abuse from my cousin as a child, then later from my mother's boyfriend, I lost faith in God. I began to believe that if neither Him nor the people that were supposed to protect me would, I'd be forced to do it myself. I became my own source of faith at a very young age. I learned later that internal resilience or "stubbornness" some may say, was something God graced me with all along.

No matter what happened to me, I always believed that something better was available for me. I guess you could contribute that to my imaginative mind as a child. As a younger sibling of a brother who was six years my senior, and cousins who were closer to his age than mine, I tapped into my ability to entertain and comfort myself with my imagination. Outside of that skill, I would be a lonely child.

Growing up in one of the worst neighborhoods in Memphis, TN, I had to believe my life would find its way beyond the hardships I saw and experienced every day. As I got older, I had to believe that God wouldn't have allowed me to suffer so much without a purpose.

I can admit, even growing up in a traditional Southern Baptist church family, there's never been a time, I can recall, that my faith has been a blazing fire, too big to be contained. Rather, I would describe it as a glowing ember that continued to burn throughout my life. Much like the remaining wood from a once burning campfire, or the subtle glow of used charcoal, my faith over time, had diminished so much that an outsider looking in, wouldn't believe there was any purpose left inside of me. However, if you're a candle lover such as I am, you'd know that even wicks that rest in candles may seem too meager to be of good use, but they can still be ignited. Their flames, though sometimes small and seemingly fragile, can be surprisingly powerful enough to fill entire rooms with fragrance.

Have you ever struggled to light a candle wick as such? It may take one a little bit of time to get it going, sometimes maneuvering the candle to a perfect position and shielding it from the slightest wind that could threaten its existence- but, eventually, it will catch on. That's what my faith has been like.

Through childhood abuse and trauma, my faith continued to burn, even if only slightly. Those were the moments I would require repositioning. And only when I felt protected from the harm that threatened my existence, would I feel free enough to allow my fire to grow.

There were not many places where those conditions favored my ability to grow, but luckily, I would find that place in school. School, for me, was not about nurturing relationships though. For one, I did not know how and two, I never felt I could relate to the child appropriate problems my peers experienced. By the time I was in middle school, I struggled with protecting my body and sleeping at night. I didn't have the capacity to care about who would be at the 8th-grade dance or doodle names of the members of B2K in my Trapper Keeper. However, I wanted to. Unfortunately, my harsh reality wiped away my ability to have those types of carefree moments.

For me, school was the place I would be able to show my worthiness through accomplishments. My grades excelled because I would always seek out who I thought to be the smartest kid in class and secretly set goals to beat them. It kept me focused, and when I succeeded, I felt validated. In the rare moments when I failed, I would simultaneously revel in awe and sulk in jealousy of my unknowing competitor. I hated and desired the idea that they got to excel in school and live happy, normal lives when they left. Thus, I forced myself to do better.

So, when I made it to college and began to fail, I lost control. I had no idea who I was without the academic success I'd planned. That was one of the moments when outside forces were needed to ignite my internal flame; a flame that I'd once before, seemingly successfully, managed to keep glowing on my own. School was the very thing that, once taken from me, forced me to acknowledge all the things that had buried my ability to experience internal joy and grow deeper connections with anyone outside of competition.

I flunked out of nursing school my senior year, and though it took me five years to gain access to and matriculate through the program, I still felt validated. Even as my cohorts passed me up and made it to graduation, I knew that in the end, when I became a Naval Nurse as a Commissioned Officer, my label of success would have been worth the struggle. I reminded myself that I was living out my success story and soon enough, I would be able to share with others how I "made it" despite the academic hardships. My path, I thought, was set.

Never mind the fact that I was not-so-lovingly labeled the problem cadet in my collegiate ROTC program. I challenged the rules in every way possible. Also, forget the fact that I had no real desire to be a nurse either. What drew me to both the military and the nursing field would be, aside from trying to prove others wrong, the security it would grant me.

Security was something I never had growing up, and it was something I desired for myself. My security and trust in family were first taken from me when I was sexually abused by my older cousin as a young girl and later blamed for my misfortune. The revelation of the abuse created temporary tension among my family that would soon be forgotten, and I would spend the rest of my childhood forced to interact and share space with my perpetrator as if nothing had ever happened. My sense of security continued to be stripped from me as I was forced to habitually move from place to place with my mother while she followed the desires of her heart, despite my brother not having to.

Lack of security and the complete demise of trust continued when the abuse made its way into my home. My mother introduced me to who would be my next perpetrator for more years to come, as her boyfriend. Unbeknownst to me, my mother was also seeking connection and security from the hurt her life had provided her. This boyfriend brought her that security, though it wasn't what she'd imagined. The security he brought to her was not that of safety and harmony but of familiarity. She had also lived a life of trauma and pain, and he would ensure it continued with him and made its way beyond her to me. I would soon be the victim of sexual abuse at the hands of my mother's boyfriend, sometimes with my mother's assistance.

Maybe I should retract my earlier statement. If ever there were a moment in life where I felt as though death was upon me, it would be the night I woke up to my mother and her boyfriend in my bed. I was fresh out of elementary school and by this time, I had only been an unwilling auditory spectator of their sexual escapades. Whether it was hearing them through paper-thin walls of our one-bedroom apartment or listening to them in the middle of the night where we shared a 2-bed hotel room when visiting family up north, I had always had a source of distraction even if it was not effective. However, this time was different. Was she drunk? High? Those were the questions I asked myself, as I laid frozen in my bed with nowhere to escape as I felt first his hands then hers violate my body.

Having outer body experiences or dissociating myself from my sexual abuse was something I had learned to do around the age of eight and this time was no different. I laid in a trance unable to move, think, or speak. I could only imagine myself outside of myself. It was as though I had front row seats watching myself starring in a movie that played out right before my eyes. When the scene was over, and their intoxicated bodies (something I choose to believe had to be a factor), left my bed, I returned to myself and became overcome with emotions.

First, it was fear. Everything I did and felt grew from the fear that seemed to be deeply rooted in my spirit. Then it turned into fear accompanied with anger, disgust, guilt, and sadness. Fear then led me to be overly protective and cautious with my body not only from Jody but, also my mother. From that moment forward, I would never again feel comfortable with a hug or a simple touch from her. Imagine living your entire childhood more traumatized by your mother's touch than comforted.

That was the night I would lose ownership of my body once again. That was also the night my body would involuntarily convulse, and I would silently cry myself to sleep, although peaceful sleep would never come, it was something I'd become used to. This was the night, having wanting to die, I recited a familiar prayer for God to kill me or deliver me.

I wish I could tell you that memories like this were few and short-lived, but they weren't. There aren't enough pages to share my stories with you here, but experiences such as these were what I had to face when school became what I thought was a dead-end. I no longer had the security of school, the influence of the military or even the distraction of sorority life to mask the hurt I'd been carrying for my entire life. With it all taken away, I was left to face my fears- Fears that the image of perfectionism, I failed to maintain, would reveal my fear of abandonment, hurt, and safety.

All of this would lead to my second round of depression because I didn't know how to handle the failure. But, even during my darkest depression, the small glimmer of faith within me had not been extinguished. It would take friends who believed in me to blow a little air onto my dying flame. It wasn't instantaneous, and it took consistency on their part. Most times, it worked. Coupled with my unwavering belief in myself and desire to want better, I would muster enough energy to re-enroll in school, after being forced to sit out, with a different concentration.

My new sense of worth would even help me to attract a relationship that I would eventually learn was as toxic as the relationships I'd witnessed from my mother. The resilience in me wouldn't allow that to dowse my faith, though it would come alarmingly close. However, when it did, more friends poured into me, filled me back up, encouraged me, and renewed my faith in myself. Their help, in those moments when I found myself homeless, hungry, and helpless were God's way of reminding me that along my journey, He'd always send what I needed to make it even a small step forward.

# *Little Girl Arise*

He never allowed me to die like I'd prayed for so many years and He didn't deliver me from those experiences of pain. He did, however, give me an everlasting wick of faith that would carry me through them all while supplying those who would become connected to me, with flames powerful enough on their own to extend to me when my faith did not seem strong enough.

Today, I bear proof that the *little girl* who was meant to die could *arise* from the very things that have kept her buried for years. I've turned my pain into purposeful healing, not only for myself but also for others who share my story. My journey is marked with incredible lows that even I cannot tell you how I was able to pull myself up. People who've heard my story always seem impressed by my strength and courage, but it's not something I ever feel justified in glorifying because it has never been me.

If it were left to me, I would have drunk myself into oblivion by now, but God blessed me with a disgust of alcohol that would deter my every attempt to drink away my sorrow. Left to my own devices, I would surely have a drug problem, but He sent a friend that would intervene in the most delicate of ways. Should I have chosen, I would have had the willpower to drive over a bridge every time I couldn't see my way out. It was never *me*. Something stronger than me pushed me in directions I didn't have the strength to go on my own.

God is real. He must be. He's been that flame in me that has always burned just enough to make me peel myself off the floor. Even now, as I share my stories of triumph over trauma, His presence will grow bigger. My faith will grow stronger, and my fire will grow into the burning inferno that will set my path ablaze leaving behind the ashes of what tried to kill me. I am Hope, an Arisen Little Girl.

## Erin Beyond the Tunnel

*"Fear not, for I am with you; be not dismayed, for I am your God. I will strengthen you, yes, I will help you, I will uphold you with My righteous right hand,"*-Isaiah 41:10

Many times, in life we may find ourselves living in fear; either in adolescence or even throughout adulthood. We may feel fear from something as minute as not knowing what lies ahead on the first day of school or even the fear of becoming bold and doing fearless things like stepping up for yourself or others. It's ironic that we find ourselves in a state of fear so often, yet God did not give us the spirit of fear. The words "fear not" are found in the bible 365 times. That is a powerful reminder not to fear because God is with us 365 days of the year. God was so intentional in the writing of His Word.

Living in fear is one of the easiest things we can do, but standing up and stepping out on faith, believing God will strengthen us and uphold us is the most fearless thing we can ever do. We allow our flesh to die, or in this case the fearful little girl inside of us to die, to allow her to arise among her circumstance and become a testament to others that God is faithful even in the darkest of times.

Five years ago, I found myself in the moment that caused me to die and revert to feeling like a little girl. I can recall lying on my kitchen floor in my nightgown screaming for my life as my husband strangled me for the first time after confronting him because of his infidelity. I was two weeks postpartum with our second child. I can still hear the screams of my oldest daughter in the background as she yelled, "Daddy stop!" I saw her in my peripheral vision attempting to use all her might to cry for help.

As I watched my little girl, I felt as if I reverted to my adolescence, in a hopeless state, with no way out. I couldn't think, let alone breathe. I couldn't even hear the words that came out of his mouth that night. I could only feel. I felt the pressure of his hand on my throat and wrist as he held me down. I felt helpless. I felt pain. Most of all, I felt fear. I feared that it would be my last night alive. I thought to myself, was this really the life that I've come to live; full of crying nights, depression, anxiety, and even suicidal thoughts.

As time passed, the abuse became the norm for me. I just didn't recognize it as abuse. After my first traumatic experience and several after, I continued to forgive my husband and showed him never ending grace. I cared more about making him comfortable and things going in his favor than my own safety. I compromised the lives of my children, my own as well, for his happiness, which seemed to be impossible. I was always doing or saying something wrong to deserve his physical and verbal responses of anger and rage.

Over time, I'd separate from him attempting to move forward, knowing that I couldn't raise my children in a place of pain and dysfunction. Not knowing what steps to take afterward and not having a rock-solid plan of escape, I'd let him back in my life over and over for years. I didn't know how we'd survive financially. I didn't have much family nearby to turn to for help, so I felt the need to fend for myself in a battle that I felt I would never see victory in. The arguments were louder, and his anger worsened as time passed. This would all happen in front of our children, and I feared for my life and theirs.

I put on a fake persona most days around co-workers, friends, and family, although most already knew what was going on. Although I was unhappy and fearful, I went about each day as if domestic violence was not my reality. I compared myself to others and felt like my situation was livable because I didn't have visible bruises or broken bones. I didn't realize that abuse was more than just physical pain. It was mental, emotional, and even financial as well.

I was belittled and talked down to. I was continually persuaded that the situation I was in was better than what most women were going through, and that this is what love looked like. If I spoke of leaving, I was threatened financially that bills wouldn't be paid. I had to learn the hard way that love wasn't being dragged like a rag doll around my own home. Love was not being reminded of every argument by the visible holes in the walls and broken doors.

I was persuaded that it'd be wrong of me to involve authorities, and I wouldn't be a loyal wife if I did. I kept silent and allowed the fear of a man to dictate my freedom and safety. I allowed this man to compromise my good judgment as a mother. I allowed others around me to discount my truth to make me feel as though what

I was going through was a part of life, and that a working husband who paid the bills was more beneficial than fighting my way to freedom.

My ignorance put me in a place where I allowed my children and I to live in an unsafe space for far too long. We feared him yet forgave him in the same breath because he was all we knew. Although I didn't truly know what love felt like, I blindly believed that my relationship with my husband consisted of love and that he cared for me. I had to learn for myself that this wasn't so, and the love God had for me is so much greater.

*"Have I not commanded you? Be strong and of good courage; do not be afraid, nor dismayed, for the Lord your God is with you wherever you go."*-Joshua 1:19.

I slowly gained the courage to express that I wanted a divorce and could no longer continue to live in dysfunction with our children bearing witness. As I spoke my truth, it was as if my words were being turned to deaf ears. My husband didn't fully comprehend a word that I was saying to him. It was as if he was in denial that I was speaking of separation and divorce. He didn't identify himself as being an abuser, and in turn, placed a lot of the blame on me. We were living aimlessly, continuing a cycle that seemed unbreakable. In his eyes, we were working things out, but I was still looking for my way out.

After yet another argumentative car ride explaining that I desired divorce, he repeated that no one else would love me the way he loved me, and that he'd done so much for me over the years. He started to speed on the high rise and close fisted the steering wheel several times ending with hitting the rear-view mirror and windshield. Once again, I feared for not only my life, but my children's lives as well. I still remember looking at their faces full of tears as they held hands in the backseat screaming for him to stop.

This moment alone was my arise moment. I felt the need to *arise,* not for my own safety, but to save my girls. Saving them meant saving the little girl inside of me. They are my heart and life source. When I saw that they were in danger, I blamed myself for allowing things to escalate as far they had. I wanted better for my family and I was going to make it happen at all cost. My children deserved to live a life that was fulfilling and full of joy, not sorrow and fear.

After his rant and expression of immense anger, my husband finally left the vehicle. I sat there in the passenger seat in disbelief of what had just taken place. Glass was shattered on the floor and in my lap. The rearview mirror swung back and forth from its wires like a pendulum as the camera blinked in a shade of green with no images to show. I didn't have time to pull myself together or even wipe my own tears. I hopped in the driver's seat and headed back on the road home silently putting a plan in place because this was the last and final straw.

*"But let him ask in faith, with no doubting, for he who doubts is like a wave of the sea driven and tossed by the wind." -*
James 1:6

I reached out to my father to let him know the extent of my situation, and that I was in dire need to relocate as soon as possible for the safety of my family. He purchased our plane tickets, and over the following two weeks I purged my entire apartment as much as I could between selling items, giving to the Goodwill, and throwing things away.

I don't remember crying very many tears as I prepared to leave behind the only life I had ever known for the last eleven years to embark on a journey that only God could prepare us for. My mindset was in survival mode. I believed that the move was in God's plan, and that every incident that happened helped lead me to this point to finally *arise* over my circumstance.

On July 19, 2018, with the clothes on our backs and two suitcases packed to the brim, my daughters and I stepped foot on the plane to head across the country with all hopes that our new life would be waiting for us on the other side. I can truly say that ever since we landed we've been covered by God's grace and favor with every step in the transitional process. This is the best decision that I could have ever made.

*"But those who wait on the Lord shall renew their strength; they shall mount up with wings like eagles; they shall run and not be weary; they shall walk and not faint."* Isaiah 40: 31

The *little girl* inside of me arose, and I'm so proud of her for regaining her freedom, her boldness, and her strength! I didn't know how I'd form an exit plan while being an unemployed freelance writer with debt and mouths to feed all riding on my shoulders, but I knew that somehow God would make a way and He did just that and more.

In this process, I wasn't thinking about trying to be brave. I was doing what was best for my little girls and myself. I didn't second guess myself or fill my mind with a bunch of "what ifs ". I was tired of covering up scars with temporary band-aids. I was ready to allow total healing to take place.

I didn't think about what wasn't on the other side, but more about all the opportunities to come and possibilities for our future. I just listened to God's call and followed His voice. I knew that God would provide. I knew that He'd carry me through those times that seemed to be unbearable. I had to let go of the fear that I held on to so dearly and allow the boldness of my faith to guide me.

God heard my prayers as well as my cries. He knew just what I needed to do to reach beyond the difficult times that I faced. He truly strengthened me from within and showed me that there are no limitations to what He can do.

I found strength in the desire to protect the lives of my children, and to let them know that their mother would never allow them to live in fear or feel forsaken. I wanted them to know that they were always going to be safe with me, and that they could find their strength as well because I pushed through a difficult circumstance with them right by my side. My children were witnesses to me choosing life. I chose to live and not die, and I'm here with feet planted on solid ground to share my truth without fear or regret.

I gained the courage to live in my truth. As detrimental as my experiences in life were, I wouldn't take them back. Those experiences, whether good or bad, are a testimony for someone else's healing. I've found my purpose in sharing my story with others. I've been able to inspire and encourage other women who have experienced similar situations to cease being their own obstacle so that they can reach higher heights and deeper depths.

We were all created with a purpose. We must be able to break through to receive our breakthrough. The only way to do this is by trusting in God's word for us and walking in alignment with His purpose for our lives. No matter the route, we will always end up right where He destined us to be.

I'll leave you with the encouraging words from an old friend. "You've come this far. Don't let anything or anyone set you back. We've lived in the darkness of our pain, the shadow of lies and secrets, the rumors and the truth of infidelity that penetrated our hearts. We've discovered that there is light at the end of the tunnel. Get beyond the tunnel and walk in the light. The tunnel serves a similar purpose to a bridge. The difference is that you came under water to get through. Your journey had the pressure of water on every side. In the tunnel it appeared dark inside even though there was light outside. You have traveled a different passage than others, but don't just get to the end of the tunnel. Get beyond the tunnel." My little girl was reassured that it was time to arise when I stepped out of the tunnel.

# Crystal's Cry for Help

Romans 12:2 (NIV) says, *"Do not conform to the pattern of this world but be transformed by the renewing of your mind. Then you will be able to test and approve what God's will is—His good, pleasing and perfect will."* Being saved and truly knowing Christ at a very young age didn't save me from all the pain and heartache I experienced trying to conform to the world. As I begin to write, I think about all the mistakes I've made, and how conforming, following my will and the ways of the world, made life so much harder for me. My story is one of decisions.

Through my story, I pray that you see that God's will is the best will. You have purpose! The choices that you make in life determines how long it takes to discover your purpose and live the life that God has for you.

"Crystal, please don't tell me that you're pregnant." Those words uttered shortly after my seventeenth birthday became the moment my life changed forever. I went against everything my parents taught me. "Crystal, you have plenty of time for boys. Boys only want one thing. If you are going to have sex, use a condom. You will not be with that boy forever. Save yourself for marriage. You're not old enough to deal with the consequences of sex. *"* Of course, all those thoughts play into my mind, NOW. Then, was another story.

When I was dating Darrien's dad, you couldn't tell me that we wouldn't be together forever. We made plans; I talked about him all day and talked to him all night. Boy do babies change things. We were great throughout the pregnancy. He talked about how he was going to be a better dad than his own. He even got a job in preparation for our unborn child. I just knew that everything would be fine once Darrien was born. I remember thinking to myself, I'm going to prove my parents wrong. He won't be like the other guys, he'll be different. Well none of that happened! Darrien was born in March. We were broken up by October. The decision to go against how I was raised backfired.

There's this thing called wisdom. When wisdom is spoken into you, receive it. Believe it or not, there are people who know something about what you're going through. It may save you some heartache or even some time. But of course, the wisdom that I'm sharing with you right now comes from some very hard lessons that I had to learn myself. Having a kid, becoming a teen mom; bad decision, right? Well it gets better.

During my freshman year at LSU, I was trying to be a successful college student with a 7-month-old baby. Do you know how hard it is to be a full-time college student? Add to that having to work as many hours as you can to support a baby.

As if I didn't have it hard enough, here comes another distraction...I met a guy that lived not too far from LSU's campus. He was completely different. He was funny and romantic, and he didn't mind that I had a son. So once again I fell in what I thought was love. Instead of focusing on my classes and my son, my focus was on him. Great decision, right? I wanted to make sure that he was happy. What is it about young women that we can become so blinded by men that we continue to make decisions that take us further away from our destiny? Well that's exactly what I did and guess what...I was pregnant again.

There were plenty of disappointed people; myself included. As if one child wasn't enough, now I had two babies to care for. At this time, I was in my junior year at LSU, close to being a college graduate with a child, and now another child was about to be added to the mix.

I lost my TOPS scholarship, my graduation date, my sanity, and eventually, my guy. Yep, months after I had Jordan, we broke up. So that leaves me single, 20, and with two kids by two different guys. That is NOT how my mom raised me. That was not what God wanted for me.

I remember the devastation this break up caused. I did what I always do, ran to God. Isn't it funny how we run to God when we are in trouble? Even though He told me to go left, I went right. And when He told me to go right, I went left. So now that I'm in a pickle, *a very sour pickle*, I run to God. I'm thankful that He's a God of grace. I knew the decisions I was making weren't God's plan for me. It's amazing how it took something so devastating to cause me to really hear God.

I moved back home with my mom and my two handsome boys and started to pick up the pieces of my life. There were many teary nights. I was determined to graduate, but to do that I had to shift my focus. I had two children depending on me. I had to make them and my mom proud. I also had something to prove. I had to prove to the world that being a teen mom doesn't stop you from succeeding. I had to prove to everyone that looked down on me that I would not be another statistic.

My first semester back, I finished my 15-hour semester with a 3.5 GPA. That spring semester, I took 18 hours. I finished that semester with a 3.0 GPA. When you remain focused, even with two little human obstacles, you can achieve what you're set out to do. I was back on track doing the things I was supposed to do.

I was so focused that on May 18, 2007, *5 years after I started,* I graduated. I received a degree, passed my licensing exams, and was ready to teach. My boys were two and five at the time. I remember thinking to myself, *I did it, I finished, life is about to get so much easier for me. I'm going to have a job. I'm going to be able to provide for my children. I'm going to be good.*

Well they weren't. Don't get me wrong, I was very successful professionally, but personally was another story. I'll never forget the year my entire grade level teaching team got engaged and married all in the same year. That was tough. At this point, I felt that marriage was the next thing. I already have the kids, now I need the husband to go with them. These feelings led me to making my next poor decision.

I went looking for a man. *God gives us the desires of our heart, right? He knows I desire a husband, so this should be easy.* I began making more bad decisions. That's what happens when you don't wait on God. Some of my decisions were so bad that they put me in a place where the people around me didn't know me, and even worse, I didn't know myself. Those years were so painful that they're a blur.

See, my way of dealing with pain was to become numb and that is exactly what I did. I was numb, ignoring my feelings and God. I remember feeling that I was already disconnected so I might as well disconnect. That wasn't a good decision. There was even a moment in my period of disconnect that I just knew my boyfriend at the time was heaven sent. Everyone was telling me differently, but I knew better. I decided that I would once again prove everyone wrong. Well, like before, that backfired.

After that relationship, I made one of the best decisions of my life. In 2012, I decided that I wouldn't let anyone, or anything allow me to disconnect from God. Yes, it took me ten years from the time that I had my first child to realize that I was going to put God first. I made that vow to Him. I began going to church faithfully and got involved in ministry. I praised, worshipped, fasted, and prayed faithfully.

During this time, I had a boyfriend, but this time, when he started to show who he really was, instead of conforming for the sake of love, I stuck with God. I broke it off with him. To this day I'm so proud of that decision. When we have God in the midst and we do things for His glory, we will always make the best choices. Now don't get me wrong, I still desired a husband, but after all the poor decisions that I made, I had no other choice but to wait on Him. I no longer wanted to do it my way.

Sometimes, God will sit back and let you do your thing. He will let you run yourself crazy and wear yourself out. It's not until then that we humble ourselves and allow God to be God, and that's exactly what I did!

It was July 2014 in Atlanta, GA at the Full Gospel Baptist Church Conference that my life began to really shift. After ministering in dance, the Holy Spirit fell heavy upon me. I remember crying a cry of surrender. It was at that moment that I realized that I didn't want *my* will anymore; I wanted to live my life fully for Christ.

I didn't want to think about a husband, marriage, a relationship, or anything related. At that moment, I declared that I would remain celibate until I met my husband. I wanted to focus on God, myself, and my sons. Nothing else mattered! It took me twelve years! As I write this, I feel the liberation that I felt at that time.

I came back from Atlanta free, and lived my life for Christ. I served in church on the dance and youth ministry. One bible study night the youth pastor asked me to teach bible study, but I didn't know I'd be teaching alongside one of the Elders of our church. I mention this because there are many women who want to know what to do while they're waiting on God; my answer is serve.

That's exactly how my husband came, *serving*. All this time, I'd been making poor decisions, and doing all these different, foolish things looking for love, not realizing that God is love and if I seek Him first, all of the things that I desired will be added unto me (Matthew 6:33).

My husband noticed me! I wasn't dressing provocatively. I wasn't dancing in the club. I wasn't getting set up by a friend. I wasn't on a dating app. I wasn't changing who I was to be something I was not. I tried all those things before to no avail. I was serving. Just like that I started dating the man that God had for me.

Of course, I didn't know that at the time. I liked his company. He was a gentleman. He was real. He had been through his own personal trials, so he wasn't about playing games. Most importantly, he loved God. I didn't say he went to church, I said HE LOVED GOD. He had a relationship with God. I started thinking to myself this *may* be a good decision.

With 2015 right around the corner, I started to pray and think about what I wanted for the new year. Even after dating at the time, my focus was still on God. At that time, I had given up on a husband and love; this man was making me change my mind, though. My prayer was for help. I had discovered myself and rediscovered God, but now I needed some *help*. My help didn't have to come in the form of a man. I was thinking a raise, some more help from my boys' fathers, another job, etc.; as usual, God had other plans.

During our Apostolic Address in January 2015, we were called to the altar. I remember going to the altar because I really didn't know my purpose or calling. I remember these words like it happened this morning. Bishop prayed. Afterwards he said, "I don't know who this is for, but your help is on the way." I cried because I knew God was talking to me.

My First Lady confirmed that my help was my husband. Shortly after that, we were engaged. We have now been happily married two years. I have the absolute best support system. I have many things beyond help. God gave me what I asked for and so much more.

My purpose in sharing my story is not to show you how to get a husband. My purpose is to empower you. It's to tell you that it doesn't matter how you start. You could start off with two children, but still earn a bachelor's and master's degree. You could still be successful in your career. You could still be put in positions to speak your truth to bless others. You must persevere. Even when things get tough because of you and your poor decisions, you use what's on the inside of you, the things that you were taught to push through.

My purpose is to tell you that God's will is the best will. You can do your will; however, it may take you twelve or more years to get to the place that God wants you to be; the place you desire to be. My purpose is to tell you even through your poor decisions, you don't have to settle. Realize that you're not your mistakes or your poor decisions. Let me repeat that because someone needs it again, you are not your mistakes or poor decisions.

My purpose is to tell you to put God before everything. Though there may be many people around us that are making poor decisions, you and I are not of the world. We do not conform, we must be transformed by looking to the hills from which cometh our help. And *His* help made all the difference. When my little girl accepted that it had to be God's will, that's when she began arising.

# *Lorna Asked, God Answered*

Years ago, I asked God to use me anyway He saw fit. I wanted my life to have meaning. I wanted to do whatever God needed me to do. I prayed that prayer and I meant it, but I had no idea that using me would come in the form of loss... a very big loss.

In 2010 I found out I was pregnant with my third child. I can't lie and say I was initially happy about this news. Weeks before I found out about my pregnancy, I'd made the decision to leave my job. I did the big jump into my purpose of writing full time...or so I thought. My family was expanding, and my husband and I hadn't expected to add another mouth to the table. Once we accepted the idea that our family of four was about to be a family of five, we were very excited. We made plans to welcome our baby girl into the world and into our lives.

Kourtney Noel Lewis made her entrance on March 21, 2011, a whole four weeks earlier than my due date. The worse day ( or what I thought was the worse day), was when I was discharged from the hospital, but Kourtney had to stay a while longer. Every day I was calling the hospital or going up there to see my baby. Being with her was the highlight of my day. I couldn't wait until the day came when she could come home to be with her father, brother, sister, and me.

That day finally came on April 21$^{st}$, a few days before Easter Sunday. The NICU doctor called and I remember his words clearly; he said, "Hello Mrs. Lewis, how would you like to take your baby home today?" I'm pretty sure the smile on my face and the joy in my heart couldn't have possibly been any bigger. Kourtney was home with us where she belonged. It's amazing how the minute a baby enters your life it's hard to imagine what you did before them. Kourtney had all of our attention. We kissed, loved, and hugged her so much. She was our wonderful little blessing, and in our minds, the completion to our family.

Most days it was still hard for me to believe that I was the mother of three. I was overjoyed that God had blessed me with two little girls. My mom passed away when I was 13-years-old, so the thought of doing all the mother-daughter things with my girls that I never got to do with my own mother was the best feeling ever. I'd already planned shopping sprees, mother-daughter trips, and all that you could imagine a mother and her daughters would enjoy. I even looked forward to the not so fun things like refereeing when Kourtney would try to take Kirsten's clothes without her permission, Kourtney wanting to follow behind Kirsten and her friends, Kirsten fussing because she wouldn't have time for her annoying little sister, and all the other drama that comes from having girls.

All my plans and dreams faded away the morning of October 9, 2012. That was the morning I woke up and realized that at some point, while we were all asleep, God sent His angel to escort Kourtney back to Him. Growing up, I was always told not to question God or His decisions, but on that morning, I ignored all of my childhood teachings. I questioned, and I questioned a lot. I wanted to know why He took her away. Why did He give her to me in the first place if I was only going to have her for 18 months? Why would He do that to me? To my husband? My children? What had we done to deserve to be hurt so badly? Nothing made sense. No matter who I spoke with, who I prayed with, who I sat in silence with, it still didn't make sense.

I can't tell you exactly when it happened, all I can say is it finally happened. The broken *little girl* on the inside of me woke up one day and felt at peace. It must've happened around December 26th, a little over two months later, because God gave me these words and I posted it on Facebook.

It's titled: **A Conversation with God!**

**God:** There's something I need you to do.
**Kourtney:** Why me Lord?
**God:** Because you're very special and the task at hand calls for a beautiful and special person.
**Kourtney:** What am I to do?
**God:** I need you to go and just be yourself. I need you to cause everyone you meet to fall head over heels in love with you. I need you to use your big personality and your big heart to touch lives.
**Kourtney:** Why am I doing this?
**God:** Because there's a family I need to use in a very important way. I need to use you to make sure they're steady

and up for all that I have for them. I need to be sure that they won't doubt Me in the time of trouble. I need to know they can trust Me even when things are at their darkest.

**Kourtney:** How long will I have?

**God:** You'll have 18 months. I know you because I created you. You have everything in you to complete this task in a short amount of time.

**Kourtney:** Won't it hurt them when I leave?

**God:** It will hurt, but I need to see if they'll trust Me to be with them. I need to see if they'll feel Me in the midst of their storm.

**Kourtney:** Will I ever see them again?

**God:** You sure will! When they've completed their tasks, I'll call them home too and you'll all be reunited again in heaven.

**Kourtney:** Okay God, I'll make you proud of me.

**God:** I have no doubt, that's why I chose you.


**We all know that she did exactly as He wanted. On October 9, 2012, she heard the words we all should be working to hear one day "well done my good and faithful servant, well done."

We're now entering the next chapter and I can't wait to see what God has planned. I know it's going to be great** :)


I have no doubt God gave me these words of comfort. He's done that before. In 2009, two years before Kourtney was born, I published a daily devotional titled The Gift of an Abundant Life. This book is a year's worth of devotional readings and here's what God gave to me on October 9, 2009.

# *Little Girl Arise*

*October 9*
**Surrender Your Heart**
**Job 11:13–14**

Surrender your heart to God, turn to Him in prayer, and give up your sins—even those you do in secret.

**Personal Note:** We're very good about giving our heart to people. We fall in love and declare that our spouse or mate has our heart. But what about God? Does He have your heart? Is He on your mind as you go throughout the day? Do you get a comforting feeling just thinking about Him? Is He the first person you want to talk to in the morning and the last person at night? **Is your love for God conditional? Do you love Him even when He takes away your loved one?** Can you say you love Him no matter the circumstances? God's love for us is unconditional. There's nothing we can do that will make Him stop loving us. Surrender your heart to God and experience what true love really feels like. Have a wonderfully blessed day.

Why did God give me that message to write two years before my daughter passed away? Do you think it's because He loves me so much that He wanted to put that message on my heart? I know that God has placed something special on the inside of me and He's always there, especially in my darkest hour, to make sure that little girl, the one who could've easily given up and turned her back on God and on life, who was broken and destroyed and wondered what she'd done to deserve that kind of treatment from God, the same little girl that He refused to leave no matter how upset I became, the one He rocked to sleep at night and gave a dose of His grace and mercy every morning when her eyes opened to see another day, God made it clear that no matter what, He had His hand on me--His little girl.

I may not know when it happened exactly, but I can tell you that one day God touched me, and He did instruct the little girl on the inside of me to arise and to go out and be an example of what faith looks like. God used me to show other grieving mothers that there's life on the other side of pain. It took me a while to understand that the burden He helped me carry may cause someone else to take their life, leaving the task undone. God needed someone strong enough, with enough faith, to complete such a big job and He chose me.

During this journey I realized I may not know all the answers, I may never know all the answers, but as long as I know He's with me and will never leave nor forsake me, then I'll continue to get up every day, and I'll continue to allow the little girl inside of me to arise and shine as she was created to.

# Little Girl Arise
## Closing

This has been an amazing journey. Yes, I know it may have been hard at times, but certainly worth every bump in the road, every detour, and every delay. If we could've changed things we would've, which is why it wasn't left up to us. God chose us to endure these painful experiences, to live through some of the most difficult moments, and to endure the most trying times because He knew we were fit for the challenge. When He created us, He added extra dosages of love, joy, peace, longsuffering, kindness, goodness, faithfulness, gentleness, and self-control (Galatians 5:22), the things He knew we'd need to complete the task He set before us. Little girls, God chose us because He knew all that He put in us would come out of us to see us through every challenge, every dark moment, and every dying situation.

Your journey of arising isn't complete here; now the true work begins as you fulfill purpose. Remember to complete your workbook activities and 60 Day Little Girl Arise to Purpose Minder. These are key components to the maintenance of your healing, deliverance, recovery, and fulfillment of purpose. It's a part of your survival toolkit. As I did to begin this journey, as well as throughout, allow me to pray with you. I ask that God seals what He has done in and through you, and after reading and engaging with *Little Girl Arise* your life will never be the same. Amazing things are in store for you, Little Girl. I can't wait to hear about your arising one day!

*Prayer*

Father God,

We, Your little girls, Your daughters, have embarked upon and completed a journey that wasn't easy. A journey that doesn't end at the close of this book, but one that is leading to our next phase of fulfilling purpose. It was quite difficult to begin, even harder to continue, but so rewarding to complete. If we are to remain whole, if we are to maintain our healing, deliverance, and survival, we need You to continue with us as we walk in the purpose You've ordained since our conception.

Many of us have faced life difficulties that we never imagined we'd encounter, then while in the midst of our adversity never thought we'd make it through, and afterwards, certainly didn't think we'd survive it victoriously. We've been victims of circumstance, held hostage by our own choices, and disheartened due to the ill will of others. We've been taken advantage of, misused, and mistreated. The love we've offered was received, but rarely reciprocated. We've sown and went the extra mile with no one ever doing the same for us. God, we've been spiritually standing and fighting as You've instructed us to; however, sometimes we've continued to feel downtrodden, defeated, and altogether disappointed.

At times we've blamed You, sometimes others, and many times ourselves. We have beat up on ourselves, been mean and spiteful to others, and turned against You. We've held on to every act against us, allowing it to slow us down and preventing us from reaching the potential You placed in us. Because of what others did, the things that happened to us, all that went wrong and never right, we've remained stuck in a place You never intended for us to be. While, yes, You allowed the storm to come, You did so with purpose; *our purpose.* You did so because You knew what You put in us and wanted to bring out of us. You did so because You knew You could trust us.

# *Little Girl Arise*

You designed Your daughters very meticulously, taking Your time to ensure that every measure of our being embodied Your strength, Your love, Your character, and Your resilience.

You created us to be like You, but somehow, we've allowed others and unwanted life experiences, to redefine who we are by what has happened *to* us.

God, if we could go back and rewrite our life stories, we'd delete all the scenes that caused us pain. We'd rewrite the moments of abuse and neglect, violence and suffering, being disrespected and taken for granted. We'd rewrite failure and disappointment, missed opportunities and closed doors. We'd rewrite loss, death, being left behind, and forgotten.

God everything You ordained, if it were left up to us, we'd rewrite it. That's why You didn't make it our decision. If we rewrote what You planned for us, we would've never experienced these things, causing us to miss out on the eventual victories we'd receive, the harvest we'd gather from seeds sown, and the lives changed because of our faithfulness and endurance. I understand now, had I not lived every life experience You placed on my path, I would've missed something; had I missed something, many of Your daughters may never be free to arise.

Though it was difficult for us. Though we screamed, cried, shouted; cursed, isolated ourselves, ran and fought. Though there were times we wanted to give up, we turned away, and we tried it our own way. Though we blamed You, others, and ourselves, we continued to stand. As we stood, somehow, someway, we willingly abandoned our will, and embraced Yours. It was not easy, and there are times it continues to be a struggle, but because You never left us and remained with us every step of the journey, we survived.

Father as we, Your chosen vessels, continue our journey, we pray to do so differently. We pray that we do so with humility yet boldness, joy and gladness; as victors not victims, conquerors not the conquered. We pray that another little girl sees us and thinks to herself, *I know if she can survive I should be able to also.* And God, not that she only thinks it, but that she does just that, survive. Use our life events for Your glory. Use it to edify the body of Christ. Use it to show Your daughters, and sons, who You truly are. Use it to manifest purpose in the earth so that all come to know You, embrace You, and recognize that they are one of Your very own.

Yes Lord, I have hurt at the cost of others, but if it means that my purpose would help, change, or save the life of someone else, God thank You for using me. Now I ask that you sustain my healing, and in moments that I want to revert, strengthen me and send support to stand in the gap. I hope that I have honored You and did what You wanted me to do with my life and this writing, and not my own personal desires. As I was transparent, I thank You for Your covering from the enemy and any attack he attempts to use towards me. Lord, I'm no longer a little girl; I've arisen.

In Jesus name. Amen.

**Also Available:**

Little Girl Arise: Workbook

60 Day Little Girl Arise to Purpose Minder

Made in the USA
Middletown, DE
27 May 2019